Advance praise for *Already There*

"Reading Mossa's book is like having a good man—a good priest—come to your home to hang out with you for a bit. Taking an honest, sobering, and optimistic look at the difficulties of his own past, he finds God in the midst of it all. Readers are left with much hope and the desire to find God in the peaks and valleys of their own lives."
—Mark E. Thibodeaux, S.J., author of *God's Voice Within*

"In our desires God speaks to us profoundly. Mossa wants us to pay a little closer attention to those desires, and in so doing to discover the ways that God has been diligently working to draw us closer to him and find our happiness."
—Tim Muldoon, author of *The Ignatian Workout* and *Longing to Love*

"With the humor and grace of an old friend, and the wisdom and winsomeness of someone who knows you better than you know yourself, Mossa weaves popular culture, spiritual disciplines, and everyday life together so naturally that you forget you're reading. I opened this book, and God found me."
—Kenda Creasy Dean, Professor of Youth, Church and Culture, Princeton Theological Seminary

ALREADY THERE

already there

Letting

God

Find

You

MARK MOSSA, S.J.

ST. ANTHONY MESSENGER PRESS
Cincinnati, Ohio

Nihil Obstat: Hilarion Kistner, O.F.M.

I Will Possess Your Heart
Words and Music by Benjamin Gibbard, Jason McGerr, Nicholas Harner
and Christopher Walla
© 2008 EMI BLACKWOOD MUSIC INC., WHERE I'M CALLING
FROM MUSIC, SHOVE IT UP YOUR SONGS, GIANT BEAT SONGS
and PLEASE PASS THIS SONG
All Rights Controlled and Administered by EMI BLACKWOOD MUSIC INC.
All Rights Reserved   International Copyright Secured   Used by Permission
Reprinted by permission of Hal Leonard Corporation

Scripture passages have been taken from *New Revised Standard Version Bible*, copyright
©1989 by the Division of Christian Education of the National Council of the Churches of
Christ in the U.S.A., and used by permission. All rights reserved.

Cover design by John M. Lucas, LUCAS Art & Design, Jenison, MI
Cover image © Masterfile Images
Book design by Mark Sullivan

LIBRARY OF CONGRESS CATALOGING-IN-PUBLICATION DATA
Mossa, Mark.
Already there : letting God find you / Mark Mossa.
p. cm.
ISBN 978-0-86716-765-8 (pbk. : alk. paper)   1. Spirituality—Catholic Church. 2.
Christian life—Catholic authors.   I. Title.
BX2350.65.M68 2010
248.4'82—dc22
2010016902

ISBN 978-0-86716-765-8

Published by St. Anthony Messenger Press
28 W. Liberty St.
Cincinnati, OH 45202
www.SAMPBooks.org
www.AmericanCatholic.org

Printed in the United States of America.

Printed on acid-free paper.

10 11 12 13   5 4 3 2 1

Do you believe because I told you that I saw you under the fig tree?
You will see greater things than these.
—John 1:50

Nothing is more practical than finding God, that is, than falling in
love in a quite absolute, final way. What you are in love with, what
seizes your imagination, will affect everything. It will decide what will
get you out of bed in the morning, what you will do with your
evenings, how you will spend your weekends, what you read, who you
know, what breaks your heart, and what amazes you with joy and
gratitude. Fall in love, stay in love and it will decide everything.
—from "Rooted and Grounded in Love,"
by Pedro Arrupe, S.J.

I have had the privilege of knowing and loving many amazing young people who have peopled my youth groups and classrooms in the last twenty years.

This book is dedicated to my "kids" because, as they are always eager to remind me, they're not kids anymore.

CONTENTS

ACKNOWLEDGMENTS

There are many people to thank for what has been a long process between the germ of an idea, and the book that has resulted. I must first acknowledge my many students and youth group members over the years who, in various ways, made me aware of the need for such a book. In South Carolina, they were members of the St. Thomas More Catholic Center, St. Joseph and St. Peter parishes in Columbia. In the Bronx, there were the students at Fordham University, which I now call home again. In New Orleans, my students at Loyola University, especially the members of Compass, who inspired me to make them the subjects of my writing on more than one occasion. Father Mark Thibodeaux helped to free the idea for this project from my hard drive, putting it into the hands of Lisa Biedenbach, who has been more patient with me than I deserve. I thank both of them for offering encouragement and helpful criticisms along the way. Rewards for patience are also due to Mary Curran-Hackett, my editor, who endured the resistance and insecurities of a fledgling book author, and made the book better. I am very grateful to her, and all the people at St. Anthony Messenger Press who had a hand in the editing, presentation, marketing, and promotion of the book, so that it could achieve its purpose by finding its way to you. Nancy Vericker offered incisive and insightful editorial suggestions—even if I didn't always heed her advice—and has been the faithful friend and believer that every writer needs. Father Jim Martin also took time from his many responsibilities as editor and author himself to offer advice on parts of the manuscript. I am grateful for that, and his willingness to go above and beyond by contributing a most gracious foreword. I've further enlisted him to tutor me in his writing disciplines, so the next book won't be so long in coming! A conversation with Clarissa Aljentera resulted in a last-minute save, for that I'm grateful. Thanks also to many others who read and reacted to various chapters: Joshua King, Michael Koch, Maggie Geene, Karen Hall, and Brian McLaren. Finally, I must thank my brother Jesuits for the many ways, large and small, in which they've supported this project especially those who helped me in various stages write this book.

Mark Mossa has a beautiful voice.

I'm not talking about his singing voice (which is perfectly adequate) but something just as important: his writing voice. Inviting, friendly, accessible, sensible, and funny, he's the kind of writer that you want to spend time with. That's an especially important attribute when it comes to writing about spiritual matters, since far too many books on spirituality are written in a high-flown style that makes you wonder if the writer ever doubted, struggled, or suffered. Mossa approaches spirituality in a remarkably down-to-earth way, showing readers how to find God in all things, as the Jesuit motto has it. And I mean all things—not just in prayer and in worship services, but in your working life, in your relationships, and even in pop culture, which, as Mossa reminds in a terrific aside is "*popular* for a reason."

There is no need for spiritual matters to be cloaked in arcane language, complicated sentences and convoluted paragraphs that you have to pick your way through just to understand what they're saying. After all, Jesus never spoke this way. More often than not, he used the form that is known as the parable. In his book *Parables in the Kingdom*, the great Scripture scholar C.H. Dodd defined a parable as "a metaphor or simile drawn from nature or common life, arresting the hearer by its vividness or strangeness, and leaving the mind in sufficient doubt about its precise application to tease it into active thought."[1] And while Dodd's definition doesn't pass the simplicity test, it gets to the point. Parables are simple stories from everyday life that make difficult concepts like "the reign of God" or questions like "Who is my neighbor?" more intelligible. Jesus understood that a story can answer a question better than a definition.

Mossa tries to do the same thing in his new book: Offer earthy stories and examples that make approaching the reign of God something for everyone, not just academics. And not just for wizened monks but for a young man or woman still struggling to figure out his or her vocation, if not identity.

You'll enjoy this book, I'm sure. What's more, I'm sure it will help you find your way closer to God. Just sit back and listen to this author's beautiful voice.

—James Martin, S.J.
author of *My Life with the Saints* (Loyola Press)
and *The Jesuit Guide to (Almost) Everything* (HarperOne)

How to Read This Book

A book always presents a certain temptation toward measuring completion. *Only fifty pages to go, and I'll be finished!* This is not a book that's meant to be finished, or measured in that way. As contrary to your reading habits as it might be, it will reward the slow reader. It will be a much richer experience if read during the course of a season, no matter if it is spring or football, rather than in one day, or even a week. Of course, if you're reading this during a retreat, that might be a little different. Time moves more slowly then. But, still, I hope you find the need to take the book home with you, or buy a copy, once the retreat is over.

Though small, this is not a book that's meant to be read in one sitting. The chapters are deliberately brief. For each one, there is a "blank" to fill in. That blank is your experience. Just as Saint Ignatius Loyola insisted on the importance of repetition in the spiritual life, you'll find a good deal of overlap, as each chapter is meant as a self-contained reflection on one aspect of the spiritual life. Each chapter serves as a sort of mini-retreat for you to reflect upon and pray upon your own experiences, perhaps even using my own experiences as a means to start thinking about your very own. As far as it is possible to finish this book at all, this is the only way it will be completed.

Years of experience, reflection, and prayer have gone into the writing of this book, yet I still know that much could be added and changed. But, I have left it to God to make use of its merits, and to make up for its shortcomings, as I pray every day he might do with me. It is my great desire and prayer that some of what is contained in these pages may allow God to do the same with you.

May the desire with which we begin our worship, also mark this beginning. The grace of our Lord Jesus Christ, the love of God, and the fellowship of the Holy Spirit, be with you!

—Father Mark Mossa, S.J.

July 15, 2009

The Feast of Saint Bonaventure

Boxes of Frogs, Mother of God

••••••••••••••| *Living the Spiritual Life* | ••••••••••••••

The truth is there are a million steps, and we don't even know what the steps are, and worse, at any given moment we may not be willing or even able to take them; and still worse, they are different for you and me and they are always changing. I have come to believe the sooner we find this truth beautiful, the sooner we will fall in love with the God who keeps shaking things up, keeps changing the path, keeps rocking the boat to test our faith in Him, teaching us not to rely on easy answers, bullet points, magic mantras, or genies in lamps, but rather in His guidance, His existence, His mercy, and *His love.*
—Donald Miller, *Searching For God Knows What* [1]

The spiritual life is about making connections. My friends tell me that I have a talent for making weird connections. As a result, this book may be a little different than what you expected. I hope it is.

My spiritual life has never come in neat little packages. No, the packages usually come somewhat damaged, despite the handle-with-care warning labels. And the contents are often not what I expected, maybe a chipped, algae green colored ceramic frog instead of that colorful tapestry of the Madonna and child I had ordered. Or some other sort of cosmic mishap that forces me to think, as cliché as it sounds, "outside the box." Thus, the need to make connections. It takes some work to figure out why I've received the frog with the yellow underbelly instead of that intricately woven Blessed Mother and child. There is some spiritual lesson in this awkward amphibian that I'm meant to discover!

But to do so I need to see things in a different way.

This book will try to help you discover this new way of seeing. It's not meant to instruct you how to see the way that I see. You have your own unique way of making spiritual connections and it is my hope that something, perhaps many things in this book will put you in touch with that. Therefore, what you will not find here is a step-by-step formula for spiritual success. That's not to say my book has no structure. It's just that instead of steps you'll find that the book is organized around one key recognition: Whether we like it or not, each of us has a past, present, and future. And that, as you might have guessed, they're connected.

Steps don't work for me because, if anything, my spiritual life has progressed in missteps, and not without stepping on a few toes— unfortunately, not just my own—along the way. Indeed, if I told you my life story, I expect you would say, "Boy, that was random," or, if you were less kind, you might cringe and say, "Boy, that was messy." But, perhaps you can relate to life being messy. And, perhaps like me, you are convinced (or want to be) that there is some meaning to all that messiness, some reason why I keep running into frogs instead of the Mother of God. I'll share a few of those messy and not-so-messy stories with you later.

For now, let me just point out a few things. The word *spirituality* has come to mean so many things that in some ways it has become meaningless. The "spirituality" section of many bookstores might include everything from Saint Augustine's *Confessions* to *Astrology for Dummies*. When some people claim to be "spiritual" they are often referring to some vague feeling that they would have difficulty describing. Some would say that this is the point, spirituality is unexplainable. There's something to that. But true spirituality must point us in the direction of living differently in concrete ways. This is the spiritual life. The spiritual life moves us beyond vague feelings into a relationship with a real God who speaks to us and works in us in real ways. That feeling you get when you sit alone in your room listening to music, or when you're at a rock concert feeling connected with the music and the crowd may be an *invitation* to the spiritual life, but it's not *spirituality* unless you act on it, unless it puts you in touch with God, and other people.

At first, when people started asking me what kind of book I was writing, I said "a spirituality book." After a few blank stares and less than enthusiastic responses, I realized that wasn't saying much. A "spirituality book," as I've noted, could be about just about anything. So, let me be more specific about what this book is and isn't. This book is an introduction, by no means a comprehensive guide, to living the spiritual life, a specifically Christian spiritual life. Therefore, this book begins with a few presumptions. The first is, as I said, that each of us has a past, present, and future which are all connected, and which are all involved in the totality of our spiritual life. Second, is that each of us is a unique creation of God. And, finally, that God took human form approximately two thousand years ago, and lived among us in the person of Jesus of Nazareth. It is not necessary that you begin this book by believing all these things, but if you find something true in what I have to say, I believe that this is only because these things were true first. Everything in this book connects back in one way or another to these foundational beliefs.

Since I will be speaking a good bit in this book about my own experiences with God and the spiritual life, I also should clarify one thing: In the course of history, some saints, and even some crazy people have shared with others that God spoke to them in an audible voice. It may be that I'm not saintly or crazy enough, but this has never been my experience. Yet, from time to time, I will speak in these pages of how God told me something or revealed something to me. This was not by means of some audible voice, but by means of images or thoughts which came to me usually in prayer, but, sometimes, simply by reflecting on my own experience, or even on a song I'd heard. So, if you're not hearing voices, it doesn't mean that God's not speaking to you. You need only take some time to reflect on your experience, and that is what this book is meant to help you to do. The more you reflect, the more you'll see that God has already been trying to communicate with you in unexpected and surprising ways.

You might have noticed that there are not many Catholic Christian spirituality books out there that speak to your own experience. I noticed that too. While there is a certain wisdom, as I have discovered, that comes from poking around in the dark and seeking guidance from some of the great spiritual masters like Thomas Merton, Henri Nouwen, Saint Augustine, and Saint Ignatius, I would have liked to find a few books that spoke more directly to the experience of being a young Catholic trying to find his or her way in late twentieth– and early twenty–first century America. Frequently, as Tom Beaudoin points out in his book *Virtual Faith: The Irreverent Spiritual Quest of Generation X*, I have found that sort of thing more often in popular culture—movies, music, television, fashion—than in spiritual books. Which left me to do the work of making the connections.

You'll find me making a lot of these types of connections in this book. This isn't just some excuse to talk about my favorite songs or movies, or some lame attempt at being hip like Pastor Skip in the movie *Saved!* saying, "All right! All right! *Who's down with G–O–D?*" Rather, it's because I've discovered that pop culture is *popular* for a reason. The images, lyrics, and oft-quoted lines that stick with us do so because they connect with something deep down inside of us—they say something meaningful about our human experience, which lies at the core of our spiritual life. But like that vague spiritual feeling I spoke of, this isn't spirituality itself, but our invitation to the spiritual life. Once we've made this initial connection, we must complete the connection by eventually making God and other people a part of it. Therefore, I invite you in this book to make all sorts of connections with some stories of the Bible, with some great saints and spiritual writers, with the teachings of the Catholic church, with yourself, with others, and with Jesus Christ through whom God made the most intimate connection with our human experience.

You may find an occasional pearl of spiritual wisdom in these pages, something you can jot down in a notebook, or share with friends. But this book is not meant to be studied so much as experienced. There will be no test on specific points in the book, and its benefit should come more intuitively, through your making connections with your own life and experience rather than by memorizing or even remembering specific points made in the book.

In the end, that package might arrive with that intricately woven tapestry which was just what you ordered, or you might receive a tacky ceramic frog. Some of you, I know, would rather have the frog. Either way, that's just the beginning. You've got work to do. But, don't despair. If you've seen the movie *Magnolia*, or read the book of Exodus in the Bible, you'll realize that even when it rains frogs—*especially* when it rains frogs—that means God is up to something!

First Love

· · · · · · · · · · | *Our Desire for God, God's Desire for Us* | · · · · · · · · · ·

How I wish I could see the potential,
the potential between you and me.
It's like a book elegantly bound,
But in a language that you can't read just yet.

You've gotta spend some time, love.
You've got to spend some time with me.
And I know that you'll find love.
I will possess your heart.
> "I Will Possess Your Heart"
> —Death Cab for Cutie[1]

From an early age, we all hope for the unique and wonderful experience of falling in love. This is not surprising. By the time we are teenagers, we have heard enough pop songs, or read enough magazines and how-to books on the subject, as well as indulged in plenty of romantic comedies (which all have the same plot, but are no less entertaining) and watched enough television dramas and comedies to convince us that, as problematic as it might be, the only thing worth having is *love*. Yet, if we look deeper within ourselves, we find that it isn't merely these environmental factors that draw us to love. Rather, this longing for love is already there. God created human beings for love—to give love and to be loved. The movie *Moulin Rouge* expresses this particularly well in the refrain: "The greatest thing you'll ever learn is just to love and be loved in return." This simple phrase identifies what in many ways is the fundamental task of a young adult. It is also the key to the search for God.

Learning this lesson isn't easy. It is an education which can bring us immense joy, but also inconsolable sadness. Many of us decide, whether we realize it or not, that it is not worth the risk. Some give up on love all together, choosing a life of self-reliance, adopting the motto, "I can do it all myself; I don't need anybody else." Others become professional "lovers," constantly giving to others selflessly, but remaining empty inside because they won't allow anyone to love them in return. To one degree or another, all of us share in this experience, finding that the longing for love inside us, while it may have lead us to ephemeral joy in the past, has also led us ultimately to enduring pain. So, our longing for love is often overshadowed by fear.

In our teenage and even young adult years, we are often free of such fears. We allow ourselves to fall in love, to find love, to be found by love. Even later, having the wisdom of experience, we affirm that there is nothing like being in love for the first time, nothing quite so wonderful. For me, at a particularly difficult time in my life, love came as a joyous surprise. When I was nineteen years old I had no idea where my life was going. The path I had originally set out for myself suddenly ended in a roadblock of financial difficulties. After only one year of college, I had to drop out. Thrown into the adult world prematurely, a world I had hoped to avoid for at least another three years, I was confused, doubtful, and fearful for my future. And the voices of those around me—"Once you leave college you'll never go back," "What are you going to do now?"—didn't help.

Then all my doubts and fears dissipated with the appearance of Christine in my life. From the moment I first saw her, I was taken. I first caught sight of her at my sister's graduation, and I thought I'd probably never see her again. However, to my great surprise, she arrived at my house later with my sister and other friends who were all going out to celebrate. I joined them, and with my sister's help as matchmaker, it didn't take long for Christine and I to find ourselves deeply in love.

This was not the only new love in my life. My interest in Christine was more than just love at first sight. I was deeply impressed by her commitment to her Catholic faith, something of which I had lost sight that first year in college. She was part of a young adult Catholic prayer group that was dedicated to prayer, praise, and song. So I became part of it too. Each week we would gather to pray, sing, and share about our encounters with God in our lives.

I received permission to attend a retreat meant for high school students, something Christine was also involved in, and soon after would become part of the team who led these retreats. My faith in God quickly became more than simply a matter of tagging along with Christine. I found myself in love again in a new way, this time with God. I had courted God since my youth, always keeping him close by, but never letting him this close. Never had I been so excited by the idea of God, and never had he been so present in my life. Amidst all my confusion, I could be with Christine, I could pray and sing and lead retreats and the combination of God and Christine made everything better.

The first year of all this was wonderful. I had never been so happy. And it was all because of God, and Christine, or was it *Christine and God?* I developed a hunger for things spiritual. I read book after book about the great things God had done in people's lives. I read the Bible. I worked full-time as a bank teller and evangelized the people I worked with. I spent most of my free time with Christine, and I even thought I might someday marry her. I was confident in God's goodness and no longer had any fear about where my life was going. I had Christine, and God would provide everything else I needed.

After about a year of this excitement and confidence, I learned a hard lesson—first love ends. One of Christine's ex-boyfriends had just ended a relationship and was making it clear that he wanted her back. This was enough stress to emphasize other tensions in our relationship, and suddenly my great love for Christine was not enough. The relationship ended awkwardly and painfully. I lost Christine and I was shattered. As there is nothing so wonderful as first love found, there is nothing quite so painful as first love lost.

Suddenly God no longer seemed so good. After all I had done for God in the past year, how could this be happening? Things were no longer clear. The "prayer, praise, and song," while somewhat consoling, was not enough to reassure me of God's presence and benevolence. I went from being sure about God to being more confused than ever. I thought surely I had found what I was looking for. It was clear I hadn't.

The crisis of first love's end comes to all of us. It is just as true of our relationships with others as it is of our relationship with God. The challenge is to allow our inner longing for love to still guide us in the face of the disappointment and pain which these relationships bring us. We recognize that first love is so wonderful, and it is, precisely because it is a love free from fear. If we are to be our authentic selves, we must find a way to love again, perhaps not without fear, but convinced that it is worth the risk.

When my first love with Christine ended, it was one of the most painful experiences of my life. Suddenly the confusion I experienced before our relationship came rushing back, along with the added doubt, whether the pain of the ending had been worth the exhilaration of the beginning. And with that the question: Why had God betrayed me?

And it was at this time that I found my greatest consolation in a song. The title of a U2 song expressed exactly where I found myself, "I Still Haven't Found What I'm Looking For." It held the strange truth that we can find pieces of what we are looking for, as I had, but that we must face the reality that they are just that, only pieces. Our lives with each other and with God resist simple formulas and are ever mysterious. Our first loves, true as they are, also tend to be somewhat selfish, so that when they end we are challenged to find a way to live that goes beyond our own selfish desire to be happy and pain-free.

God can speak to us through a pop song just as powerfully as he can in prayer, if we are willing to listen. So I listened. The song described a longing very much like the longing for love I had discovered before. The song expressed the great desire just to be with *you*. But the song, at least to me, wasn't addressed to some earthly lover. Its lyrics mentioned the kingdom to come and the one who carried the proverbial (or literal) cross, which suggested that perhaps the song was expressing a desire to be with God, especially in the person of Jesus Christ. It spoke plainly to me that my belief in God didn't provide all the answers, but that *being* with God was the answer to some fundamental need.

I came to realize that this song not only expressed what I was feeling, but it was an expression of the experience of many. The title aptly expressed the main spiritual experience of all of us, at any age, who are still *searching*. The words of the song communicated the desire that drove us, even if we hadn't put it into words. All that we were doing, that we were searching for, whether we realized it or not, was contained in the refrain of the song. The song described running, crawling, scaling walls, all in the pursuit of this one goal: to be with *you*. In this pursuit we don't have to have everything figured out, we can believe and still be unsure of the path we need to take. This, I realized, was a song not simply of searching and confusion, but of deep spiritual desire, a song which echoed the tortured song of my own heart.[2]

I can still hear this song regularly on radio stations today and it is a testament to its continued appeal and to the truth which it expresses. The *Catechism of the Catholic Church*, far from the dry, uninspiring rule-book it is often characterized as, tells us, "The desire for God is written in the human heart."[3] This is a reality for all human beings. But, as I found out in those difficult days of my early adulthood, at no time is this reality more apparent and more pressing than in young adulthood. Saint Augustine, in the midst of his own young adult faith journey, wrote of our relationship with God: "To praise you [God] is the desire of man, a little piece of your creation. You stir man to take pleasure in praising you, because you have made us for yourself, and our heart is restless until it rests in you."[4] If we stop to examine ourselves amid the manic activity and confusion of our young adulthood, what we will find is a heart that in the midst of our many advances, regressions, and mistakes along the way is driving us to run, crawl, or do what ever it takes to be with Christ, who is our heart's desire.

Thus, to speak about a spirituality for young adults is to speak about a spirituality of desire. The goal of that spirituality is nothing more—and nothing less—than to be with God. And, as the song suggests, there are many paths to get there, but our challenge is to find the unique path that God has laid out for each one of us. With varying levels of awareness, we are all walking this path. But to discover what it is we are looking for it is not enough to set our sights on being with God in some ideal heavenly future. The spiritual life requires an appreciation of how God is with us where we are now and where God was—or wasn't—with us in our past. It is by means of this journey of awareness of self-with-God, and with God-in-others that we can better learn to love and be loved and more completely realize our desire to be with God in all the places where our lives take us.

Living in Palookaville

········ | *Already There—Letting God Find You* | ·········

I kept my faith, even when I said,
"I am greatly afflicted."
—Psalm 116:10

If those hypothetical aliens that people are always talking about were to visit Earth (if they haven't already) and study the human species, I would guess that alongside observations like, "Humans have two eyes, stand upright, are prone to war, and have an odd fascination with celebrities," might be the notation: "They never seem to be happy where they are"—cross-referenced to "odd fascination with celebrities."

It seems almost against our nature to be happy where we are, and probably to a certain extent it is. For were we not somewhat restless, were we not uncomfortable with staying too long in one place, we would not find the drive, the desire, to discover and create new things, and we would not look outside ourselves in search of relationships to enrich and improve our lives and offer us the reward of love. Yet, amid this restlessness, if we are not able to find some appreciation for our lives at this moment, we will miss out on the graces available to us in the here and now, and never find the peace to which God invites us. One of the first challenges of the spiritual life, therefore, is to appreciate where we are, even if it's not where we want to be.

This isn't always easy. Sometimes where we are just plain sucks, and we are hard-pressed to find anything to appreciate about it. We've all been there. Our friends might even reassuringly recognize: *Yeah, it sucks to be you right now!* There are a number of temptations when we reach this point. We can feel sorry for ourselves and tell everybody about how awful our life is. Though soon those friends that so aptly recognized our plight might also tell us: *It sucks to be* around you *right now, too.* We can deny that things are bad and invent for ourselves a fantasy future in which all will go our way—*everything will be fine when that person of my dreams comes to take me away from all this, or when I win the lottery.* Or we can become obsessed with past failures, missed opportunities, and injustices we've suffered which, had they not happened, would have made things turn out far different for us today. No one of these is any better or worse than the other, but each gets in the way of accepting who we are at this moment, and acknowledging that God might have a reason for putting us here.

* * *

In today's consumer culture, which constantly bombards us with possibilities, our difficulty can become not that we place our hopes in some *fantasy* future, but that there are so many other things that we actually *could* be doing. In high school and college we find that there is a club or organization for almost every interest, and some of us (like me) try to squeeze as many of these things as possible into the limits of our "free" time. Sitting at a university graduation recently, I listened as they introduced each of the students who was receiving a special award. Sure, some nice things were said about what a great person he or she was, but I was struck by the fact that the bulk of it involved listing the many organizations and clubs that person had been involved in for the past four years. There wasn't a single award-winner who hadn't been involved in at least five, if not ten different organizations.

One could get the impression that we were rewarding quantity rather than quality. Should we really, I wondered, be praising what appears to be over-involvement? Was there no reward for the student who had devotedly given his or her time to just one or two things in an exceptional way?

I've seen for myself how paralyzing all these possibilities can be.

I've been there.

I was that student who, when high school and college was finished, was praised for all the things I'd managed to do during my time at school. I saw many different attractive opportunities before me, and I wanted to be able to do them all, so I found out all that I could and figured out how I could best juggle many at once. This could make things pretty frantic at times, but at least I wasn't missing out on anything! This is the fear which I think drives many of us—the fear that if we don't do everything, we might miss out on something good. So we sample this and that, looking for the thing that will make us most happy. But like the toy we just had to have as a child and then got bored with and discarded just days after receiving, we find that none of these things, exciting as they may be for a time, seems to be able to offer us lasting happiness.

The turning point for me came when, after returning and finishing my college degree and then still restless again after three years of attending graduate school, I was seeking yet another new thing to do. I'd discovered an opportunity to live in Japan for a year and teach English, and was looking into it. About that same time I received a call from my friend Meg. Meg had been to one of the other Catholic parishes in town and told me that they were looking to hire someone to coordinate a new program in youth and young adult ministry. She thought I would be perfect for the job. I dismissed it at first. I was happy at the parish I'd been attending and enjoyed volunteering in the youth ministry program there. Besides, the job opportunity in Japan looked pretty promising, and, to be honest, was far more exotic and appealing than doing something that I was more or less already doing.

That's when I had this crazy notion: *Maybe God was trying to tell me something?* All the signs pointed in that direction. After all, the job offer wasn't at Meg's usual parish. She just happened to go there that weekend and saw the advertisement, and thought to call me. I already had the experience and the qualifications to do the job. So, without thinking much more about it, I decided I should at least check out the parish, and apply for both opportunities to see what would happen. The program in Japan was run by a religious order, so both my interviews were with priests. I'll never forget my interview with the priest about the Japan program. It was only fair to tell him that I was at the same time applying for the other position, though nothing had yet been decided. At the end of the interview he said something very surprising. He said, "Mark, I'd really like for you to come work for us, but I'm pretty sure you're going to get that other job and you're going to take it. If for some reason it doesn't work out, I'll look forward to hearing from you."

I hardly knew how to respond. How could he know what I was going to do, when I didn't? Indeed, if you'd asked me just then I'd have probably told you that the odds were that I would have been headed to Japan. But, in the end, things happened just as he predicted. When I was faced with the choice of either job, I felt God was steering me toward the less exotic one, despite the strong pull I felt in the other direction. Meg and that priest saw something that I hadn't seen, at least until I stopped to appreciate where I was in my life. I didn't have to go overseas. I didn't have to travel very far at all. I was *already there.*

I was nearly twenty-eight years old then. So admittedly, I was a bit long in getting there. The first ten years or so of my adult life were spent bouncing from one thing to the next, supposedly looking for the thing I would give my life to, but never really giving anything my all, because in the back of my mind was the thought that there might be something even better on the horizon. I went to school, got a fellowship to go overseas, went to school again, took interesting jobs and worked at them for a time, until I got bored and something more interesting came along. Once, I sat down and calculated that I'd had about twenty-two different jobs in ten years! Sure, it was fun. I had a lot of great experiences and met lots of interesting people, not to mention developed a wide variety of work skills. But despite all this wisdom of experience, I realized that my life wasn't really going anywhere. And I only noticed this because I stopped all that bouncing around, stopped thinking about all the other things I could be doing, and took the time to take a hard look at where I was. I was also blessed that God put Meg and that priest in my life to help point me in the right direction. The key to the future, I discovered, was not in all those things outside of me, but within me, in the true yearnings and desires God had placed in my heart (not the yearnings and desires I had mistaken for them), not in the strange wonders of some far-off, exotic country.

· · ·

We can make similar mistakes with regard to the past, deciding that we were meant to do something that is no longer possible and that, since that opportunity was denied us for some reason, our life is now worthless. Consider one of the most famous movie monologues of all time. Recently, an American Film Institute poll dubbed a line from it, "I could've been a contender," the third greatest movie line of all time (after, "Frankly, my dear, I don't give a damn," from *Gone With the Wind* and, "I'm going to make him an offer he can't refuse," from *The Godfather*). It's been imitated in everything from *Looney Tunes* to 1980's *Raging Bull* to 1993's *Robin Hood: Men in Tights*. You've probably heard it, even if you didn't know where it was from. It's from the 1954 Budd Schulberg movie script *On the Waterfront*.

The main character, Terry Malloy, played by Marlon Brando, is a failed-boxer-turned-dockworker whose brother Charley, played by Rod Steiger, is a lieutenant to a corrupt union boss, and who himself has been involved in some of the union's dirty dealings, most recently as an accessory to murder. Terry comes under the influence of a Catholic priest who has made it his mission to fight the corruption at the docks. Hearing of Terry's connection with the priest, the union boss sends his brother Charley to see what he is up to, and to even kill Terry if necessary. It is during this tense meeting that Terry and Charley argue. Terry complains to Charley about his failed boxing career. Charley suggests that his brother's failure was his trainer's fault, for which Terry corrects him with the famous line, "It was you, Charley." Terry reminds Charley of the night of one of Terry's biggest fights, when Charley came to him and told him to throw the fight because the union put their money on Wilson, his opponent. Terry laments his decision to do it, because as he says, "I could have taken Wilson apart that night." Terry knew he could have won the fight, but he helped his brother out and threw the fight. Wilson went on to win the title and all Terry got was a "one-way ticket to Palookaville," he says. Brando brilliantly portrays the broken Terry and cries, "It was you, Charley. You was my brother. You should've looked out for me." Charley interjects and reminds Terry that Terry saw some money in the deal too. Frustrated with his response, Terry continues angrily, "I could've had class! I could've been a contender. I could've been somebody. Instead of a bum, which is what I am. Let's face it." After a pause, his voice lowers to an exhausted whisper and Terry says, "It was you, Charley."[1]

I was familiar with parts of this monologue, especially that last part, long before I ever knew exactly what it was about or where it was from. It's something that, even fifty-five years removed from the original film, has become part of our cultural consciousness. Public figures and stand-up comics (as well a few of us, when we're hamming it up) invoke it freely, declaring in their best breathy Marlon Brando voice, "I could've been a contender." There's no need to explain the reference. They know that many, if not most, in their audience will know what they mean. Even if they don't know the original context, they know the sentiment behind it.

This is precisely why I think a scene like this gets stuck in our collective consciousness, because we know the sentiment behind it. We've felt what it's like to have something that should have been ours taken away from us, often for reasons we had no control over. Some of us are able to move on, chalk it up to fate or bad luck, and put it behind us. But, many of us, like Terry, find it hard to just accept it, and the memory of what we "could've been" stays with us and becomes most present to us at those times when things are most difficult, the times when we don't like where we are. Here's where knowing the context of this quote is helpful, because in the monologue Terry is speaking a truth he may not have realized before. He's been going along with things for years, playing patsy to a corrupt system because he believed his chance at being anything better had been taken from him when he took a dive that day for his brother's bet. Now his encounter with the radical priest and the beautiful young sister of the murdered man has helped put him in touch with where he is and how he might be better. He may have gotten that "one-way ticket to Palookaville," but that doesn't mean he has to be a bum living there. His lament to Charley, the one who "should have looked out for" him, is the beginning of appreciating where he is and, having arrived there, to really start to live, even if it is in Palookaville.

This might seem a little strange. How does complaining about where he is free him to live his life? Well, he's not just complaining. He's putting the truth out there and confronting his brother, the person responsible, who Terry feels should have been the one to make sure that it didn't happen. He's also being honest about who he is and where he finds himself. He has turned out to be something of a bum, but he also sees that's not all Charley's fault. He's allowed himself to be the victim, and this is Terry's signal to Charley that he's not going to be content being the victim any longer.

Appreciating where we are doesn't mean ignoring the past and pretending everything is awesome, as we're sometimes made to believe.

No, the freedom to live our life comes in recognizing where we are, in all its glory and misery and accepting that reality. Accepting that reality doesn't mean that we're content just to leave things the way they are. Indeed, it is the catalyst for change, freeing us to see the truth and redirect our lives.

•　•　•

This is not some strange psychobabble, but an insight that has deep roots in our Jewish and Christian tradition. For if the endurance of some cultural artifact like a movie scene in our collective consciousness is a sign that there is something there that speaks to the heart of human experience, then we must take note of what are arguably the most enduring and, indeed, popular prayers in both the Jewish and Christian traditions: the psalms.

No other book of the Bible has as consistent a place in our prayer and worship as does the book of Psalms. There is a reading from the psalms in almost every Mass Catholics attend, the daily prayer required of monks and priests throughout the world is founded in the psalms, and among the final words Jesus spoke as he hung on the cross was a verse from psalm 22: "My God, my God, why have you forsaken me?" (Matthew 27:46).

If you've found these words of Jesus troubling, as I have, consider what some of the other psalms have to say: "Why, O LORD, do you stand far off? / Why do you hide yourself in times of trouble?" (Psalm 10:1); "To you, O LORD, I call;/ my rock, do not refuse to hear me, / for if you are silent to me, / I shall be like those who go down to the Pit." (Psalm 28:1); "For you are the God in whom I take refuge; / why have you cast me off?" (Psalm 43:2); "Has God forgotten to be gracious? / Has he in anger shut up his compassion?" (Psalm 77:9); "You make us the scorn of our neighbors; / our enemies laugh among themselves. / Restore us, O God of hosts; / let your face shine that we may be saved." (Psalm 80:6–7). "For my soul is full of troubles, / . . . I am like those who have no help, / like those forsaken among the dead, / like the slain that lie in the grave, / like those whom you remember no more, / for they are cut off from your hand" (Psalm 88:3–5). These disturb us too—are we *allowed* to talk to God like that?

Many of us find these troubling because we have been led to believe either that to complain means that we lack faith, or that we are not supposed to speak to God in anger. Well, if either were true, I expect that the people who collected together the books of the Bible certainly would have thrown some, if not all, of the psalms out! The psalms are nothing if not brutally honest.

Let's consider psalm 44 more at length. Listen to the words of the psalm. What is the speaker, if not angry?

In God we have boasted continually,
  and we will give thanks to your name forever.

Yet you have rejected us and abased us,
  and have not gone out with our armies.
You made us turn back from the foe,
  and our enemies have taken spoil for themselves.
You have made us like sheep for the slaughter,
  and have scattered us among the nations.
You have sold your people for a trifle,
  demanding no high price for them.

You have made us the taunt of our neighbors,
  the derision and scorn of those around us.
You have made us a byword among the nations,
  a laughing-stock among the peoples.
All day long my disgrace is before me,
  and shame has covered my face
at the words of the taunters and revilers,
  at the sight of the enemy and the avenger .

If we had forgotten the name of our God,
　　or spread out our hands to a strange god,
would not God discover this?
　　For he knows the secrets of the heart.
Because of you we are being killed all the day long,
　　and accounted as sheep for the slaughter.
Rouse yourself! Why do you sleep, O LORD?
　　Awake, do not cast us off for ever!
Why do you hide your face?
　　Why do you forget our affliction and oppression?
For we sink down to the dust;
　　our bodies cling to the ground.
Rise up, come to our help.
　　Redeem us for the sake of your steadfast love.
　　　　　　　　　　　　　　　(Psalm 44:8–16, 20–26)

This is a typical pattern for many of what are called the "Psalms of Lament." They begin in praise of God, remember the great deeds God has done in the past, and then remind God of the promises he has made. What follows is a series of complaints to God about where the individual or the people as a whole find themselves, the cry of a people to their God who is supposed to take care of them at a time when it seems he hasn't. We can hear in it the same frustration and anger as Terry Malloy's appeal to his brother Charley to look out for him. This is a frustrated reminder to God: *Once you told us we were special and that you would take care of us. So why do we find ourselves instead a bunch of bums?*

All the psalms aren't like this. Many are devoted to praising God and thanking God for all the wonderful things he has done and is doing in the lives of his people. But I think if we take them all together the psalms are an effective guide for what it means to appreciate where we are. Things aren't always bad. Indeed, they're frequently quite good. And some of us—and I know I'm one of them—are much better at appreciating where we are when things are bad, rather than when they are good. When things are good we just kind of glide along and enjoy it, perhaps never stopping to see what God is doing for us, allowing things to be that good. The psalms are a reminder to all of us of the necessity of constant prayer, the need to stop each day to look around and honestly see how things are going, and to share that with God. Sometimes this will mean happily offering our thanks to God for the people and the opportunities God has placed in our lives at this time. Other times, it will be that plaintive and even angry cry, "God, you're supposed to be looking out for me. You mind telling me, then, why things suck so bad right now?" That's OK too, as Psalm 116 says, "I kept my faith, even when I said, 'I am greatly afflicted'" (verse 10). Complaining to God is not a sign that we don't have faith, but that we do!

The lesson I draw from my experience is that if we get in a habit of moving restlessly from one thing to another, trying our best not to miss out on anything, it can become a justification for a pattern of escapism. *If I don't like where I am, I can just go somewhere else and start over.* In my own life story that meant attempting to move halfway across the world! But isn't it interesting that what I discovered was that God wanted me to stay right where I was, in my own version of Palookaville. And isn't there a lesson in the fact that others in my life seemed to see that much more clearly than I did? How often do we discount the insights and advice of others, thinking: *How could they possibly know what I want or what I'm meant to do better than I?* But they do, as I discovered! And that's why God puts them in our lives. Yet we can even practice a sort of escapism when it comes to them, writing them off when they tell us something we don't want to hear, or if they try to get in the way of us making the wrong decision. All serious spiritual people have others who act as spiritual directors or mentors for them. For often we are too close to things to appreciate where we are on our own. If we try to act as a mirror for ourselves, we are too close to see anything clearly. But if we let someone else we trust act as a mirror for us, then we can step back and see everything clearly.

As *On the Waterfront* continues, we see that Terry's confession to his brother is not just that plaintive cry of frustration, but the sign of transformation. If we pay attention to the symbolic nature of Terry's character, as he goes on to defy the corrupt system, we might see another biblical parallel. His appeal to Charley is like Christ's appeal to God in Gethsemane when he expressed how troubled he was by the suffering he would have to endure in the completion of his mission. Yet it is in this apparent moment of weakness, "let this cup pass from me;" where he finds the strength to fulfill his mission, "yet not what I want but what you want" (Matthew 26:39). So, too, in his complaint to Charley, Terry's own "agony in the garden," Terry finds the strength to stop being a bum and stand up for what is right, even if he has to suffer for it. And with the help of the tough priest who isn't afraid to be brutally honest with Terry, he is able to see his potential for good. There is no escape from Palookaville, but now, having come to appreciate who he is and the truth of where he finds himself, Terry discovers that he can have class living in Palookaville and be a contender, though not in the way he once imagined. The same was true in my experience. It wasn't until I stayed in one place for a while and learned to appreciate where I was that I really became a "contender" in my relationship with God. And the thing is, whether things are good or bad, once you've lived in Palookaville long enough, you find not only do you have to start appreciating where you are, but you also have to start contending with where you've been. And you might discover in your quest to find what you've been looking for that you are *already there*.

Taking the Scary Bits Out of the Freezer

•　•　•　• | *Acknowledging Where You've Been, Without Freaking Out* | •　•　•　•

> I don't know if anybody can be converted without seeing
> themselves in a kind of blasting annihilating light, a blast that
> will last a lifetime. . .
>
> —Flannery O'Connor, *The Habit of Being*,
> *"Letter to 'A,'"* January 21, 1961[1]

We've all been places to which we'd rather not return. I don't know anyone who's had a perfect life, or a perfect family. And let's face it,
acknowledging where we've been also involves considering those that
have been—or haven't been—there with us, and frequently that means
family. Terry can say to Charley, "You was my brother. You should've
looked out for me," because Charley is his brother, and thus has a special obligation to be there for him. Contending with our past means
contending with the ways in which our family has failed us (often in
dramatic and permanently damaging ways) and how we, in pursuit of
our own selfish desires, have failed them.

Most families you know are probably much like your own, to varying
degrees involving some mixture of happiness and unhappiness, each in
its own way. It seems almost a requirement that every family have at least
one "black sheep" or "crazy uncle." These days, the word *dysfunction* is
almost presumed as a complement to the word *family*. All families seem
to have their share of it. The best-selling book of all time, the Bible, is

filled with stories of dysfunctional families. One of the most famous of those stories is one told by Jesus, about a man who had two sons.

If you've ever heard the term "prodigal son," this is the story it comes from. It's the story of a wealthy man with two sons who owns a great estate with many servants. The older son is dutiful and does whatever his father asks. The younger son is more of a slacker, out to enjoy life. One day, the younger son goes to his father and asks for his inheritance in advance. He wants to travel and see the world. Now, as you might imagine, this is a pretty disrespectful thing for a son to do. Some say it would be the equivalent of saying that his father is dead to him. Perhaps there was an argument, though Jesus doesn't tell us that. Nevertheless, the father agrees to give his son the money.

He takes the money and travels to distant lands and soon uses up all his money on drinking, women, and dissolute living. Broke, he finds a job feeding pigs. He doesn't make a lot of money, leaving him hungry, so hungry that the pig slop starts looking mighty tasty! These thoughts bring home to him how low he has sunk. He thinks of returning home, but is hesitant because of the shame of what he did to his father. Yet, he thinks, "How many of my father's hired hands have bread enough and to spare, but here I am dying of hunger!" (Luke 15:17). He decides he will return home, acknowledge his sin before his father, and ask to be received back as one of his servants. And so he sets off on a journey back home.

Facing where we've been in our lives is much like the prodigal son's facing the prospect of going home. The pain or the shame of going back might seem unbearable. We might be more content to feed pigs rather than to consider how wrong we've been, or even how good we've had it. The weight of the past can seem too much for us. After all, the past is past, what good comes from dwelling on it? That's what we say. And, often the environment we live in—our families, our friends, our society—encourages this attitude. *Don't bring us down by digging up the past* is often the spoken or unspoken rule. Indeed, they might add, *don't bring yourself down.* We are encouraged to forget the bad stuff and focus only on the good moments (as long as doing so doesn't make us feel worse about the bad stuff). But it's not just external pressures that discourage us from acknowledging our past. We ourselves do a pretty good job of losing ourselves in the "pig slop" of everyday life, so as to avoid unpleasant memories.

This temptation lasts a lifetime, but seems especially strong in early adulthood. As we appropriate our new adult identity, we are inclined to think that the experiences of our childhood and youth no longer matter. This is also a time when the pains of childhood and adolescence are still very close to us. We'll deal with them, we tell ourselves, when we've gotten more distance from them, when we're more mature. The irony is that failure to consider the effect that the past can have even on our adult life might prevent us from achieving maturity. Forgetting where we've been can open the way for a certain blissfulness and allow us to have uninterrupted fun for a time (like the prodigal son's experience of dissolute living), but it gets in the way of lasting happiness.

Consider the end of Jesus' story. The young son returns to his father's house, probably practicing his speech the whole way: "Father I have sinned against heaven and before you; I am no longer worthy to be called your son" (Luke 15:21). But the father, seeing him from a distance runs out to him, embraces him and kisses him, dresses him in his finest clothes, and announces a party to celebrate his son's return. Jesus seems to be saying that while the journey to acknowledging our past might be difficult, it is worth it, and that God's love, represented by the father, will sustain us.

But that's not the end of the story either. As if to remind us that, while worth it, it may not turn out perfectly, Jesus tells us of the reaction of the older son. As you might expect he is angry, and we might even say justifiably so. He's shown to his father all these years loyalty that his young brother mocked by his actions, yet his father has never thrown him such a party. The "black sheep" of the family is being rewarded for squandering his inheritance, while the good son is being taken for granted. The younger son, while forgiven by his father, will still have to work to reconcile with his brother. Contending with our past, and with our family's part in it, is an ongoing process.

. . .

In an episode of the hit TV show *Friends*, the dim-witted Joey is trying to read Stephen King's horror novel, *The Shining*. The problem is that he's not making much progress, because every time he reaches a scary part, which is probably about every few pages or so, he jumps up and throws the book into the freezer. At this rate, there is little hope that Joey will ever finish the novel because, if anything, it's just going to get scarier and scarier.

We often treat our past lives in the same way. If we take time to reflect on our past experience, we often just on focus our good experiences—the times we did things right and the times the right things were done for us and to us. If we even look at the bad stuff that happened it is more often, like in the case of Terry Malloy in *On the Waterfront*, out of a certain nostalgia for what "could've been" if that misfortune hadn't befallen us. When we get too close to the scary parts, close enough to consider what impact that they might have on us now, often we, like Joey, jump up and store that memory deep in some freezer within our soul. We think that this will be the end of it, that having put it in "deep freeze," we needn't concern ourselves with it again. Yet, here we can take a cue from Joey's experience. If Joey doesn't take the book out of the freezer and keep it out even through the scary parts, he'll never complete the story. In the same way, we must take the risk of thawing out the scary bits of our past—the times when we've been wronged or done wrong ourselves—otherwise we'll never know the complete story of our lives.

The scary truth that we frequently want to deny is that in ways both positive and negative, our past has an effect on who we are, what we do, and how we act. Sometimes that's a good thing. If you were brought up to be polite, you'll probably continue to be polite and people are going to appreciate that quality in you. On the other hand, if you were brought up in an atmosphere in which the only time anyone ever took any notice of you was when you did something wrong, then you probably see yourself as someone who's not worth the positive recognition. People might even ask you why you are so hard on yourself.

Consider a simple example. A married couple I know once shared with me that the first fight that they had in their marriage was over how to fold the towels. They each had been brought up in a household in which towels were folded in a certain way. They didn't know there was any other way to fold towels. If something as simple as how your family folded towels can be part of who you are today, imagine the lasting effect that habitual ways in which your family members and peers deal with each other—and other more traumatic physical and emotional experiences—can have on who we become. A common experience in adulthood, and a healthy one, is coming to the realization that not everyone does things the way you did when you were growing up.

Yet, aware as we may be of the psychological power which our past can exert on us, still many of us arrive at adulthood, lock those experiences deep inside of us, and act as if our life began at eighteen. I know I did. I figured now that I was an adult, I could handle it. I wasn't going to let something that happened in the past have control over me. I was stronger than that. Sometimes we don't even know we are doing it. For years I was, and still am at times, the kind of person who would never ask other people for help, unless for some reason I was forced to. I tried to do everything myself. People would offer to help and I would say, "No, thanks. I can handle it." I didn't want to put anybody out. This sometimes got me into overwhelming situations which, if I'd only asked some people to help me, could have been avoided. One day, realizing finally that this self-reliance wasn't always the best approach, I asked myself why I was this way. I looked around and realized that most of the time people were happy to help with things, and usually they weren't put out by it, or demanding anything in return. And, here's where I had my realization. Growing up, when I'd asked for help from people it rarely came without strings attached. The person helping would tell me how put out they were by it, demand something in return, or afterward never let me forget it. In my youth, this was more often my experience than not. No wonder I was afraid to ask people for help! But then I realized, out here in the real world, especially in the Christian world in which I spend a lot of my time, this wasn't how things worked. It's still a scary thing to ask people for help sometimes. I'm not always sure I can trust them, but I can't tell you how much better my life has become since I've become less afraid to ask others for help.

An old adage says that the devil is most powerful when he convinces people he doesn't exist. The same could be said about the power of our past. The more we deny its existence the more power it has over us.

* * *

I don't write this as some oh-so-mature-spiritual-guru-who's-got-it-all-together trying to tell you how you can be like me. On the contrary, my hope is that you'll make a better start at adulthood than I did. I'm writing from my experience of screwing these things up. When I was in my early twenties I thought I was that guy who had it all together. I carried around that persona, and many people even bought it, and encouraged it, and even complimented me on my maturity. But I was clueless about the depths of doubt and insecurity that hid under my supposed "all-together" surface. I had no idea of the motivations, rooted in my past, that actually drove much of what I said and did. At the time, I didn't think there was anything so bad that I needed to see a shrink about it. I was a nice guy, appreciated by many. I was successfully completing college, knew something about having a relationship with God, and was active in church. I was a leader in a prayer group and helped lead retreats for young people, where I met another steady girlfriend,

Sarah. Thinking that I was past the initial hurt of my first love with Christine, I tried to move on and even thought I had found true love again. I achieved what I considered at the time stability in my life. But still, for reasons beyond me then, I was restless.

As much as I knew myself to be in love with Sarah, I did not feel that I could make the commitment to marriage, though we dated for several years. Sarah thought she was ready, and was frustrated by my reluctance. I couldn't "commit," as they say. We often laugh knowingly at such a comment, because experience seems to show that a comment like this is often true for certain people. Some of us do have commitment issues. But, true as it seems, such a statement can also become a convenient excuse. Blaming our fear of commitment for a failure in a relationship or on any other superficial reason for that matter, can become a means of avoiding having to ask the deeper questions: *Is there another reason why a relationship isn't working? Or why I am not growing as an individual? It there even another reason behind the reason that " I'm afraid to commit"?*

I could be a bit disingenuous and say that the reason I was afraid to commit was because, *obviously,* God had other plans for me. But that would be rationalizing and dodging the real issue, something we all are adept at doing. It's much easier to engage in a sort of revisionist history, chalking things up to fate, or God's providence. We often say things like, "If that didn't happen, or if I didn't make that decision, I wouldn't be where I am now," instead of taking the "scary bits out of the freezer" and realizing that it is the memory and pain of past experiences of being hurt by others that is really holding us back. Perhaps God did have something to do with things not working out between Sarah and me, but that's not why I wasn't able to fully commit to that relationship. The real reason was that I was afraid.

I'm pretty sure at one point or another Sarah confronted me and asked me, "What are you afraid of?" And I can say honestly that I really had no idea what I was afraid of, or even that I was afraid. I answered with something vague like, "I'm just not ready to commit to marriage yet. I want to be sure that it's the right decision, one I can make for life, and I'm just not sure about that right now." I had locked the memory and hurt of past relationships down deep inside of me and decided that the past had no effect on who the adult me was. I didn't even think that I needed any help, because I would never have considered the possibility that my reluctance to commit had something to do with my past. But I was wrong: I did need help and my past did matter. I have since learned the only way to reduce the harmful effects of the past on who I am today is to acknowledge that the past matters and affects who I am and why I do the things I do, even if I am not willing to admit it. Once I admitted this to myself, I was then able to remedy some of the dysfunction that resulted. As with any dis-ease, the only way to treat it is to know the source of it.

· · ·

For some, arriving at this point will involve some psychological counseling. If something is getting in the way of you living your life effectively, or having successful friendships and relationships with others, I recommend seeing a counselor. The insights of this book might start you along the way, but it cannot provide the continual support that you need for such a journey. But for all of us, time spent in reflection and prayer, especially with extended periods of silence, can be of great help in this regard. Not everyone has this luxury, but if you can carve out a few minutes of time each day for silence, I recommend it. My breakthrough came during the course of a thirty-day silent retreat. I realize not everyone can make a thirty-day retreat, but for me it was transformative.

My thirty-day retreat was based on *The Spiritual Exercises* of Saint Ignatius of Loyola, founder of the religious community to which I belong, the Society of Jesus, commonly referred to as the Jesuits. Like myself, and perhaps this is one of the reasons why I like him so much, Ignatius was a man who didn't get off to the best start in his adult life.

He was ambitious, reveled in being a man of the court, fancied himself something of a ladies' man and managed to get himself in enough trouble from time to time that his influential family sometimes had to bail him out. It is even believed that he may have fathered a child in his youth, but he and his family managed to cover this up. His conversion did not come until his mid- to late twenties, and it took a near-death experience to change the direction of his life. At the beginning of Ignatius' autobiography, in which he refers to himself in the third person, he describes himself this way: "Up to his twenty-sixth year he was a man given over to the vanities of the world, and took a special delight in the exercise of arms, with a great and vain desire of winning glory."[2] Now, this may not sound so bad, except that Ignatius goes on to explain how his vanity and desire for glory had some undesirable results. At twenty-six, Ignatius was a soldier in a unit of the Spanish military engaged in a battle with the French at Pamplona, Spain. He and his fellow soldiers were well outnumbered and they were talking about surrendering. But, Ignatius, not happy about the idea of surrendering, gave a rousing speech which convinced the others to fight on. They did so admirably until their confidence was shaken when Ignatius was hit by a cannonball and seriously injured, after which they surrendered.

Ignatius nearly died as a result of his injuries, but eventually managed to recover. During the course of his recovery, he asked for some things to read, hoping for some romantic stories filled with beautiful ladies, chivalrous men of the court and the pursuit of glory. There were none of these, so instead he got a book on the lives of the saints and another on the life of Christ. As he read about the lives of holy men like Saint Dominic and Saint Francis, he found himself getting excited and discovered in himself a desire to be like them, to do the kind of things they'd done. And, furthermore, he found that this desire was even greater and longer lasting than his desires for the glories of his past life. He asked God's forgiveness for the sins of his past, and became determined to live a new life in the service of God.

At this point, I imagine that Saint Ignatius might have thought this the end of that pesky past life of his. Indeed, he would soon come to see himself as a "pilgrim," getting rid of his fancy clothes and starting to wander around in ratty clothes, even letting his hair and fingernails grow and probably looking something like Jack Sparrow of *Pirates of the Caribbean*, without the mascara. Yet, despite looking like a pirate who's fallen on hard times, and giving up his life of privilege, if you read Saint Ignatius' autobiography, you can see that he didn't immediately shed all the baggage of his past.

First of all, there was the question of his health. In addition to nearly dying from his war injury, the bone didn't heal properly, leaving a rather unsightly bulge sticking out the side of his leg. You might remember that he said he was somewhat vain. Thus, he didn't like the idea of running around with a protruding bone, and asked to have that part of the bone cut off. Now, you can imagine the pain involved in such a procedure, but when he recounts it in his autobiography he explains, "He determined, nevertheless, to undergo this martyrdom to gratify his own inclinations. His elder brother was quite alarmed and declared that he would not have the courage to undergo such pain. But the wounded man put up with it with his usual patience."[3] I've always seen this part of the autobiography as rather telling because to me it says that not only was he given over to vanity when he was twenty-six, but when he is recounting this story some twenty-five years later it's clear that he's still not immune to a little bit of vanity. Even the saint, now superior of one of the fastest growing religious orders in the world, still hasn't quite gotten it all together. That means there's hope for the rest of us. It also is a reminder that whether we like it or not, our past is always with us.

Interestingly, that hint of vanity might also tell us something else. I would guess that remembering some of the skills that made him a good soldier also helped Ignatius to be a good superior to the thousands of men who joined the Jesuits during his lifetime, but drawing on those good skills meant, perhaps, that they came with a little bit of the vanity attached. So, another reason for not entirely letting go of our past is that there's some good stuff there too. It is helpful to look to the past to see that much of what is there is neither wholly good nor wholly bad, but maybe part of the reason we are tempted sometimes to throw it all away is because even the good stuff comes with baggage. When we take it out of the freezer to thaw, we have to thaw the bad and the good, because in the freezing process it's all kind of gotten stuck together.

It was during his time as a pilgrim that Saint Ignatius wrote *The Spiritual Exercises*. The *Exercises*, then, are not just a retreat guide, but a collection of Saint Ignatius' insights on the development of his own young adult spirituality. Much of the *Exercises* involves reflection on the life of Christ, because Saint Ignatius believed that by walking with Christ through his life, through the Gospel stories, we could learn much of what we needed to learn about living the kind of adult life we are meant to live. However, before we could do that, we had to spend the first week of our four-week retreat dealing with something else—sin. And Saint Ignatius knew where most of the sin in his life lay, the same place where it does in our lives—in the past. Imagine that. Back in the sixteenth century, without the benefit of modern psychological theory, Saint Ignatius, like others before him, had already discovered that we can't move forward in our lives without dealing with the past.

· · ·

I would discover the same thing in my first year as a Jesuit "pilgrim," as I began my own journey through *The Spiritual Exercises*. Those thirty days would be spent in silent prayer and for literally almost the entire first week I was going to focus on one thing—sin. I couldn't imagine how I could spend an entire week on that topic! And I can't exactly say I was looking forward to the possibility.

The song "Change" by Tracy Chapman asks us to think about this: If this was your last day alive and you were about to see God, would you, she asks, "change"?[4] That's more or less how the first week starts. First,

Saint Ignatius advises that we come to know how much God loves us and so almost every retreat based on *The Spiritual Exercises* begins with something like Psalm 139 to remind us of that:

> O LORD, you have searched me and known me.
> You know when I sit down and when I rise up;
>   you discern my thoughts from far away
>
> . . .
>
> For it was you who formed my inward parts;
>   you knit me together in my mother's womb.
> I praise you, for I am fearfully and wonderfully made.
>
>   (Psalm 139:1–2, 13–14)

And, then, one of the first meditations that Saint Ignatius suggests is to pray about your own death. If you consider the thoughts that go through your mind when the airplane you're flying in hits heavy turbulence, you know something of what this prayer might be like. Things you haven't thought about in years suddenly pop into your head. Now, imagine a week of that sort of thing with nobody to talk to about it but God, and no in-flight movie or chatty fellow coach passenger to distract you from it.

There were many things about the reality of sin that I found myself meditating on during that week—sins I'd committed, sins that had been committed against me, and finally, the sins of the world. At first, this exercise overwhelmed me, and I felt a strong temptation to flee. But I believed that God loved me, that he would be with me in this retreat, and that there was a reason for going through this process. So I tried to be as open as possible, and eventually God revealed three important insights that changed the way I would ultimately live my life. The first was that there's sin in this world, and it's impossible to avoid. It's in many activities, institutions, organizations, corporations, relationships, political parties, and even civic groups or governments and, whether we like it or not, we're all a part of it. That doesn't mean we are necessarily at fault for it, or even support it, but we are implicated nonetheless. As citizens of a complex country like the United States, chances are the country and the people in it are responsible for some sinful things, whether it's killing, enslaving, or discriminating against its own citizens or those of other countries in war situations (in the past or present) or even allowing people to die by not offering aid—in and outside the country. I have to face the fact that sometimes my country does sinful things to help ensure the quality of life to which I'm accustomed. There may be some things I can do to change that, but in many ways it's out of my hands. All this depressed me, but in my prayer to God, he showed me that I wasn't completely helpless, and there was something I could do. I felt God explain to me that the sin in the world is the result of someone, even me, choosing not to love. Imagine the impact that we individuals could make by a simple choice: Where once we had chosen *not to love*, we now chose *to love*. And what if we encouraged others to do that—it could have an amazing ripple effect. This was Mother Teresa's genius. Her message was simple: Choose to love whomever you find in need, and it will change both your lives. If enough people just did that, we could start to beat back the overwhelming power of the sin in our social and political structures that seems impossible to combat.

During that week I also asked God to show me how I needed to grow to be a more complete and less sinful person. The answer, which came to me in one of my prayer sessions one day, was just one word: *intimacy*. At first I thought, "God, could you be a little more specific?" But it wasn't long before contemplation of that one word brought to my prayer images of my past. There were the times when people had pretended to be interested in being my friend only so they could be cruel to me. There were the times when people had feigned friendship in order to take advantage of my talents, being nice to me so that I would help them with their homework or to pass a test, and then instead of thanking me, ignored me afterward. Then there were my supposed best friends who were sincere in their friendship until they abandoned me for a more popular crowd. Finally, and most profoundly, there was the pain of losing my first love.

None of these experiences, of course, are unique to me. Everyone has them; you too can remember your own past hurts. As a result, you might discover, as I did in that prayer, that because of these experiences you have adopted a pattern of not letting anybody get that close for fear that you might be hurt by them. As I looked back on my past life, I saw what God wanted me to see: I'd let fear of intimacy with others—and with him—prevent me from entering fully into my relationships with friends, family, and God. I also realized, as I was considering the possibility of a life lived in service to others as a Jesuit, that I would not be able to make that commitment unless I were able to risk opening myself up to others in their need, risking pain, but also opening the way for love. This was the reason that I wasn't able to commit to Sarah, and it was also the reason that my relationship with God was mainly an intellectual one: I hadn't yet let God, or too many others, into my heart. The challenge of my retreat largely would become, in the words of one of the Bible passages I prayed on, to remove my "heart of stone" and replace it with "a heart of flesh," one open and vulnerable to the needs of others, and the loving action of God (Ezekiel 11:19).

Finally, I realized something about how sin had operated in my life in the past. This fear of pain had not only caused me to avoid intimacy, but had also caused me to engage in a pattern of sin which I was somewhat aware of, but had not really recognized. As many of us do, I had always taken solace in the fact that I was basically a good person. Most who knew me would have said that of me, though they might have added that they didn't really feel they knew me that well. I didn't really *do* anything particularly bad or sinful most of the time. The greater part of my sin, I realized, lay in the things I had failed to do, especially in my relationships. I could see how, for example, for fear of getting hurt or hurting the other person, I hadn't always been completely honest. I avoided bringing up unpleasant things most of the time, and failed to let go of relationships that I should have let go. I wanted to avoid the pain associated with such a decision or with a relationship's end. This was perhaps my greatest sin in my relationship with Sarah, and with others who came after her. I would keep quiet and act as if everything was fine rather than face the pain of dealing with the difficulties, and the guilt of having hurt her if I did.

Sometimes what we convince ourselves is a desire not to hurt another is really more selfish than anything else. It can become a pretense for our own avoidance of a painful situation. We're not really thinking about how painful it will be for the other person, but rather about how unpleasant it will be for us. If we really examined the situation, we'd find that the other person will be hurt far more in the long run when it becomes clear (and it always does) that because we have been silent about our concerns, or our realization that a given relationship has no future, we've been going through the motions instead of facing up to the truth.

If we dare go further in examining things, we may also discover that we don't just do this to others, but we also do this to ourselves. We lock up our past sins in that freezer so that we can deny the truth about ourselves. But in so doing we shut away an essential part of who we are. Recalling Joey's dilemma, you can imagine that *The Shining* is going to be a pretty boring story with all the scary parts removed. So, too, the story of our lives. Our lives needn't become a horror story, but they can't be a one-dimensional sentimental novel either. That may be a happy distraction, but it's not real life.

.   .   .

After this weeklong meditation on sins—especially my own—I was feeling pretty weak. But feeling weak, I realized, isn't just the unpleasant consequence of unloading the scary parts of our past, it's the whole point. Saint Paul speaks of being made perfect by weakness, because it is only by acknowledging our weaknesses as well as our strengths, that we can be complete. Still, this acknowledgment isn't going to happen overnight or even in a week of silent prayer. Once we begin to remember our past sins and to acknowledge our weakness, we have to continually work at it, going deeper and deeper a little bit at a time and recovering our true selves.

Acknowledging our weakness also makes us more capable of a crucial practice of the spiritual life—compassion. Because the spiritual life opens us up to God and others, compassion is an essential part of it. To have compassion means to feel, or more precisely, to suffer, with another. If we cannot acknowledge the sin and the weakness of our lives, both past and present, it will be impossible for us to be compassionate. We will live isolated, lonely lives, never really connecting with other people, or God. This is not how we are meant to live. God became human in Jesus of Nazareth in order to show how weakness, compassion, and being with others are integral to what it means to be human. Jesus, though able to do so, never used his power as God for his own gain. He experienced material poverty, hunger, and weakness, and counted on his friends, not his own power, to provide him with what he needed. He continually railed at the powers of his day for being more concerned with following the rules and taking care of themselves than having compassion: "Let anyone among you who is without sin be the first to throw a stone" (John 8:7). And he showed us in his own embrace of weakness, to the point of suffering death on a cross, how that lack of compassion can result in great evil when the innocent suffer.

If the God who became one of us saw the necessity of accepting weakness and suffering in order to be fully human, doesn't that tell us something about what we're meant to do? It's easy to accept this intellectually, but hard to live it. We'd much rather find a way to live the spiritual life while keeping the scary parts of our past locked away. For many of us, acknowledging and accepting all of our past may be one of the hardest things we ever do, especially if we have things buried so deep that they are not immediately within reach. But the insights of psychology, the experience of Jesus and the saints, and the stories of the Bible seem to suggest that this is a necessary step. Indeed, I don't believe that it's possible to advance in the spiritual life without it. If we truly desire to know what the God who loves us desires for our lives, we not only need to pray, but we also need to be able to look at the entire story of our lives. That means opening up the freezer and thawing everything out. We might even need an ice pick for the more stubborn bits. But, in that process we may also begin to see some indications of where God might want to find us in the future.

CHAPTER THREE

"You Got Somethin' That None of Us Have"

• • • • • • • • • • | *Do You Know Where You Are Going?* | • • • • • • • • • •

> When God calls, God gives a new name. Abram became
> Abraham, Jacob became Israel, Saul became Paul, and Simon
> became Peter. We must search for this new name because the
> new name reveals the unique vocation given to us by God.
> *Compassion.*
>
> —Henri Nouwen, *Seeds of Hope*[1]

Now that you've thought about where you are and where you've been,
do you have any idea where you are going? Maybe you haven't thought
much about it. Maybe you think about it a lot. Or maybe you just don't
know what to think about the future. It's too uncertain: Who knows
what could happen? Perhaps you've had the experience of making plans
for the future, only to see everything spin out of control in another,
unanticipated direction. That person you thought you might marry
wasn't the person you thought he or she was, or like me, was unable to
commit. The job that you thought was perfect for you was given to
somebody else. Maybe you flunked or dropped out of school, or maybe
you're thriving, but there are so many things that attract you that you're
not sure what to do.

At some point most of us find ourselves paralyzed by our choices—
we either seem to have too many or don't seem to have any. Do we have
a choice when it comes to our future? The answer to this question isn't

as simple as it might seem. This is one of those annoying questions to which the answer seems to be yes and no.

We are brought up, especially in America, to see ourselves as living in the land of opportunity, which some of us think means that we can do whatever we want. It's true that there are lots of opportunities out there, but they're not really all for us. First of all, while we may be practically free to do anything that we are capable of doing, legally we are not. There are rules and laws which, if we break them, can lead us to being punished, deprived of many of our freedoms, and even confined to a small jail cell. So, while we are free to do all sorts of things, many of those things are an abuse of our freedom. Even if you're trying to make a point, running naked through Times Square is probably not going to be seen as a legitimate use of your freedom. These limits on doing whatever we want, I hope, are fairly obvious to you.

What is not so obvious, especially to the most optimistic and idealistic among us, is that when it comes to what we are going to do with our lives and what we will make our career or vocation, our choices are limited. No matter how hard I train, even should Tom Brady be suddenly forced to retire, I am just not going to be the starting quarterback for the New England Patriots next year. That's not true just because I'm in my forties. It wouldn't have been any less true twenty or twenty-five years ago. I am no star quarterback—or even a superhero like Spiderman for that matter. And, unless I am bitten by a genetically enhanced super spider, or endure some other fantastic or miraculous occurrence, I never will be.

Consider the freedom that such a realization provides. It allows us to stop chasing those unreasonable—even impossible—goals because we realize they're unattainable. And most importantly, we are forced to acknowledge that perhaps while we are not cut out for scaling tall buildings in red spandex suits, we may in fact, be good at any number of other things, and most importantly, we may discover what God wants us to do—what we were *meant* to do all along. But how do we discover such a thing?

We've already started on our way to this, by learning to appreciate where we are now, and where we've been in the past. If we look honestly at our lives, it's not always so difficult to see what we are and what we are not capable of doing. Our present circumstances offer us only so many options. I, for example, can't hop on the next plane and move to Paris—I have obligations as a priest, teacher, and student. Some of us, even without work, school, vocation, or familial obligations, can't do it either, because of financial or health issues. There can be any number of reasons why we can't do what we want to do. There are also other reasons—our own personal limitations, if you will, that preclude us from some of our dreams. Though some of us may have dreams of being the next famous supermodel or movie star, our looks or our talent might prevent us. How many hundreds of thousands of young people wait in line to audition for *American Idol*, for example, who can't even sing a note, but who no less have the dream of becoming a famous singer? There are things about our physical appearance that we can change, however, such as our fitness level. But, if we can't get off the couch or even go for a walk, chances are we won't be climbing Mt. Everest soon no matter how badly we want to or dream to do it. There are still other blockades that prevent us from pursuing our dreams and, if we're painfully honest, they are mostly self-built. To mix metaphors now, remember those scary bits of the past locked in our freezers? They may hold the reasons—whether we like it or not—for who we can and cannot become. If we get stuck psychologically or emotionally in the past and if the experiences and traumas of our past life seep into our present one, we can be limited—by fear, disillusionment, and hopelessness. Some of us, like me, may not be able to commit, move on, or even develop meaningful relationships—or find our "dream" mate, for example, even if we badly want to find one, because of the giant walls we've built around us.

For hints about our future, what we can do is look back on our past experiences to discover what patterns we might find. Is there a certain type of work that you seem to keep returning to over and over again? Have you had a lot of jobs that have put you in contact with teenagers, or with the elderly, for example? Perhaps you never realized that, without even intending it, you've been using your free time to do the same types of things over and over again. Perhaps it's not the people so much as the field. Do you see yourself repeatedly being involved in things having to do with literature or science? In other words, what are those things that you find that you have been and continue to be the most passionate about? Notice I didn't say *good* at. You may be very good at something that you're not meant to do at all. In all these things, both in your limits and your passions, what do you see God saying to you? This is where you'll find the clues to what God wants for you, *your vocation*. In the spiritual life, vocation is not just a job, or just something you do. Rather, as Pope John Paul II's biographer George Weigel once put it, (I paraphrase) it is something you just *are*.

•   •   •

There is also another, and perhaps more difficult, adjustment that is required, made more difficult because it's strongly countercultural. You see, we tend to think that the thing we are meant to do is the thing that makes us most happy. That's only partially true. You may have noticed that in previous chapters I have spoken about *appreciating* where you are, and *acknowledging* where you have been, and how that frees us for personal transformation. What I never said is that we are necessarily meant to always be happy with where we are, where we've been, or even where we eventually end up. In the end of *On the Waterfront*, Terry Malloy isn't necessarily any happier than he was, but he does have the peace of knowing that by changing his life's direction he is becoming that person with class that he had once convinced himself he couldn't be.

This is a challenging adjustment to make to our perspective, because as comfortable as we might become with it, others will not be. There is something threatening about people who are content with not being happy all the time. But the truth is that we can spend all our lives doing things that make us "happy" (the definition is fluid for some of us and for some of us the word *happy* is synonymous with *pleasure* alone) and we end up living a life that's meaningless. If we don't find ourselves unhappy at least some of the time, if not much of the time, we are probably not living a meaningful life, and certainly not living the life that God wants for us. Does that mean that God wants us to be unhappy? Not exactly. But God knows—and, in fact, Jesus told us by his word and by his life—that if we are doing what God wants we are *not* going to be living a 24/7 funfest.

Now you wouldn't be normal if you didn't find yourself resistant to this idea. And I know that this goes against what you might have heard from that televangelist's show you accidentally landed on when you were surfing channels late Saturday night (or early Sunday morning). But whom are you going to trust? Him or Jesus? A few years back, one of these televangelist types even wrote a book called *The Be-Happy-Attitudes*, which actually seems in some ways to go against the spirit of the Beatitudes (from which the name was taken), a collection of some of Jesus' basic lessons for the spiritual life. For example, it seems to me that most people's first inclination is not to be happy when Jesus says in the Beatitudes, "Blessed are you when people revile you and persecute you and utter all kinds of evil against you falsely on my account. Rejoice and be glad, for your reward is great in heaven, for in the same way they persecuted the prophets who were before you" (Matthew 5:11). Check out the prophets sometime—frequently, they are *not* happy people. They are passionate about God and doing what God wants, but they are often at the same time unabashedly miserable. Consider Jeremiah, one of the youngest of the Old Testament prophets, who in the midst of living his vocation complains:

> O LORD, you have enticed me,
>   and I was enticed;

> you have overpowered me,
>> and you have prevailed.
> I have become a laughing-stock all day long;
>> everyone mocks me.
> For whenever I speak I must cry out,
>> I must shout, "Violence and destruction!"
> For the word of the LORD has become for me
>> a reproach and a derision all day long.
> If I say, "I will not mention him,
>> or speak any more in his name,"
> then within me there is something like a burning fire
>> shut up in my bones;
> I am weary with holding it in,
>> and I cannot.
>
> (Jeremiah 20:7–9)

Jeremiah finds that, despite his unhappiness, despite the temptation to throw in the towel, he cannot escape the passion within for doing God's will. Jeremiah's complaint is a powerful expression of the desire for God that is inside each of us. He expresses in an honest way how that desire and acting on that desire has little to do with how happy it makes us. Even if it makes us miserable sometimes—as it clearly does Jeremiah— that burning fire in our bones that yearns to be in relationship with God cannot be held back.

* * *

But even if we've gotten past the happiness obstacle, there is another obstacle that confronts us—being special. I don't mean special in a politically correct "we-can't-say-unusual-or-weird" kind of way. I mean special as in unique. Everybody thinks they want to be special, but when someone finds out how special he or she really is, often he or she quickly discovers a great desire to be like everybody else.

One of my favorite TV shows was *Buffy the Vampire Slayer*. The early episodes opened up like so: "In every generation there is a Chosen One. She alone will stand against the vampires, the demons and the forces of darkness. She is the Slayer."[2] *The only one of your generation*; well, you can't get much more special than that! Some might think: Wow, Buffy's a pretty lucky girl, with all those special slayer powers. But it's clear from the beginning, and throughout the series, that Buffy doesn't think so! Indeed, Buffy, it seems, would prefer if she could just be a normal high school (and later college) student, have a normal boyfriend (one who's not a vampire), go to the mall, and drink coffee at Starbuck's like everybody else. In one episode, a young man who's just watched Buffy slay the vampire that was about to attack him says, instead of "thank you," "But, you're just a girl." To which Buffy replies, "That's what I keep saying." Key the opening theme. Buffy wishes she was "just a girl," but, like Jeremiah, no matter how much she might wish to abandon her special role, she can't deny it. If she doesn't fulfill her role as the chosen one, vampires won't get slain and her hometown of Sunnydale will go to hell, literally.

Now, Jeremiah and Buffy are some pretty heavyweight examples. Few of us are going to find that we are uniquely chosen to fight evil or to preach death and destruction to those who have turned away from God. But we all have unique talents, and sometimes those talents might threaten to take us away from the comfortable little world we've built up around ourselves. Consider a more "real life" (though fictional) example from the movie *Good Will Hunting*. Will Hunting is a tough guy from South Boston who also happens to have amazing intellectual gifts. Yet, he spends most of his time hanging out with his childhood friends and working manual labor jobs. However, one day he is discovered by an MIT professor who wants to help him put his talents to work. Will, however, is not sure he wants do that. He would rather just do what he's always done, hang out with his friends, just work to get by, and be nobody special. As he's trying to figure out what to do, he and his friend Chuckie have a conversation while working on a construction site. Chuckie asks Will if he is going to take the new job offer. Will replies that he doesn't want to be a "lab rat" and instead would rather spend the rest of his life in the old neighborhood with Chuckie and all of their childhood friends. Chuckie is visibly upset by Will's revelation. He even threatens Will, albeit jokingly and colorfully, that he will "kill" him if he doesn't make something more out of his life. He says to Will, "Listen, you got somethin' that none of us have."[3] Chuckie realizes his friend's talent, even if Will doesn't want to admit it himself. Will doesn't want the burden of being special. He would rather just be like everyone else. But, Chuckie reminds Will that he and his friends never had and never will have the opportunities Will has because of his gift. "Tomorrow I'm gonna wake up and I'll be fifty and I'll still be doin' this. And that's all right 'cause I'm gonna make a run at it.... It'd be... [an] insult to us if you're still here in twenty years."[4] Chuckie sees in Will what Will can't see for himself—his potential, his gift. Chuckie doesn't have what Will has, and like every good friend does, Chuckie pushes his friend to realize this—even if it means Will may have to someday leave the 'hood. Chuckie even admits: "But you know what the best part of my day is? The ten seconds before I knock on the door, 'cause I let myself think I might get there, and you'd be gone. I'd knock on the door and you wouldn't be there. You just left. Now I don't know much. But I know that."[5]

This scene illustrates what the stories of *Buffy the Vampire Slayer* and Jeremiah the prophet also do. Each one of us has something that no one else has. Each one of us has a unique role to play in God's plan. Our task is to discover what that is and, as scared as we might be to move beyond whatever comfortable "normal" life we've established, to act on it. And like Chuckie reminds Will, this isn't just something we owe to ourselves; this is something we owe to our friends, to other people, to God.

Notice, too, that this isn't just some typical Catholic guilt trip. Chuckie is pretty blunt with Will, but not because he wants to make him feel bad, but because he's his best friend, and he wants Will to make the most of his life, even if it means not having him around anymore. We all could use a friend like Chuckie, a friend who doesn't just selfishly hold on to us, but is willing to let us go so that we can make the most of our lives. This is another reason God calls us to intimate relationships, so that we can be loved unselfishly. It's also so that we can do the same. No matter what unique vocation God might be calling each of us to, intimate, unselfish friendships are something that we are all called to. Who knew you could learn so much from two tough guys from South Boston?

While these are nice examples, perhaps you don't have the looks of Matt Damon or Sarah Michelle Gellar, the brains of a Will Hunting, or the brawn of a Buffy; maybe you don't have the sense of being uniquely chosen out of your generation, and, if you're like me, maybe you're not feeling up for preaching death and destruction like Jeremiah. But, then again, everything that seems ordinary from your vantage point would be considered extraordinary by others. And, if you look hard enough, or from that other person's vantage point, you might discover the extraordinary in your seemingly ordinary life.

* * *

I spent my first year of college doing the same thing most kids do their first year of college—going to class (most of the time), drinking a lot (but mostly on weekends), and avoiding church. My grades turned out OK, I made a few friends, and I was even an editor on the school's newspaper. But, as I look back, the year wasn't much of a success. I failed as a pledge in a fraternity; I was passed over for a management position on campus; and I nearly killed myself (accidentally) after a night of heavy drinking. To top it all off, a shortfall of financial aid made it impossible for me to return.

After I left that college and soon after met Christine, I became involved in the Catholic charismatic movement, a movement within the church that, like Pentecostal churches, placed a lot of emphasis on the work of the Holy Spirit. It was dynamic and exciting, filled with boisterous prayer, praise, and singing about God and life in the Spirit. Its practitioners even jokingly referred to themselves as "charismaniacs." Charismatic spirituality was kind of like a superhero spirituality, complete with "superpowers" like speaking in tongues, healing, prophecy, wisdom—the gifts of the Holy Spirit. The difference was that these weren't just given to some "chosen one," but were offered to one degree or another to everybody.

Suddenly, God, through the power of the Holy Spirit seemed much more immediate. My life seemed supercharged with his presence; I was aware of God like never before. Prayer took on a new power and potential, and I felt like a major player in the great spiritual battle between good and evil. With the help of others in this community of charismaniacs, I became immersed in my faith in a powerfully new and exciting way. If I can be slightly anachronistic, I felt like Buffy Summers, Will Hunting, and Jeremiah all wrapped into one. It was, as people are apt to say where I come from, *pretty awesome.*

For me, this was something of a Catholic equivalent of what many Protestants might call being "born again." As stories of superheroes and prophets often demonstrate when we learn that we have powers that we didn't realize we had, or discover a heretofore unrecognized talent that needn't come by means of some supernatural or extraterrestrial event, we find it necessary to rethink our lives—past, present, and future. As with being "born again," our lives take a new and unanticipated direction. This is what happened to me. Suddenly I was spending much more time with my newly discovered religious friends and girlfriend, and I was also spending much more of my time doing religious things. Though my parents were Catholic, this seemed to them to be going a bit overboard. They wondered if I'd become part of some deviant Catholic cult.

But my days as a Catholic superhero were short-lived. As seems inevitable, the pain of love lost again, and other ordinary cares of life, soon crowded out the extraordinary. My days as a charismaniac, as much as they bolstered my faith, soon proved, like so many of the jobs I'd had, another fleeting distraction of which I grew tired. The prayer, praise, and spiritual gifts which at first seemed so appealing more and more became just a matter of going through the motions. Even the extraordinary spiritual gifts of God's Holy Spirit, to which I had been introduced could prove to be yet another distraction from seeking what God really wanted for me. So, I found myself again, as after my first year of college, on the lookout for something better.

I should clarify, lest I be misunderstood, that it wasn't that I found something wrong or unchristian about my involvement with the charismatic movement. Indeed, I continue to be thankful for the ways in which it reenergized my faith. The gifts of the Spirit are real and promised to us by God, though there is the danger that some, in their enthusiasm, may claim for themselves gifts that they have not been given. The problem was that, though it was having a positive effect on my faith, it wasn't helping me to discover my vocation, what God's desire was for me.

This brings us face-to-face with another surprising reality—that legitimate and even beneficial religious activities and practices can actually get in the way of finding or pursuing the future that God wants for us. In his autobiography, Saint Ignatius tells of just such a difficulty. After his conversion, his "born again" experience, Ignatius spent several years as I described earlier as a "pilgrim" speaking with others about the things of God, writing *The Spiritual Exercises,* and leading people through them, and trying to discern what God's will was for him. Yet the religious authorities of his day, the famous Inquisition, argued he had no training to do the kinds of things he was doing. Eventually, the Inquisition demanded that if he intended to continue doing this kind of ministry, he must attend school.

Ignatius complied with their request, but ran into a problem. By this time, Ignatius was accustomed to experiencing mystical visions and insights quite frequently. As he set about trying to do his homework in those early days of his studies, his attempts at memorization were overtaken by a flood of mystical insights, stronger even than those he had in prayer. It's hard to say that legitimate mystical insights of the kind that Ignatius had were a bad thing, but Ignatius concluded that despite the positive insights, the timing of their arrival was off. It seems paradoxical, but Ignatius eventually determined that in order to follow God's will for his life, he had to forgo these spiritual gifts, at least when they interfered with his studies.

Saint Ignatius is not the only one to have such experiences. All of us can fall into the temptation of doing religious things instead of finding out what God wants us to do with our lives. People that claim to be "spiritual but not religious," then, are onto something. But it's not that the spiritual life is a replacement for religion. Rather, it's that religious practice absent reflection on one's gifts and talents, one's interior life and relationship with God, one's past, present, and future in light of God's love and God's will is hollow, no matter how sincere. It's far easier to go through the motions of religious practices than it is to do the hard work of looking at your life and discovering in it what God is inviting you to do with that life. And, indeed, it is hard because many of us can't imagine that God would be so concerned with our individual lives. The famous Christian philosopher, Søren Kierkegaard, once described our relationship with God as follows:

> [T]his human being exists before God, may speak with God anytime he wants to, assured of being heard by him—in short, this person is invited to live on the most intimate terms with God! Furthermore, for this person's sake, also for this very person's sake, God comes to the world, allows himself to be born, to suffer, to die, and this suffering God—he almost implores and beseeches this person to accept the help that is offered to him! Truly, if there is anything to lose one's mind over this is it![6]

God is intent on, as Chuckie is with Will, showing us that each of us individually has got something that none of the rest have. Each of us is gifted by God with unique gifts and talents that simply fulfilling our religious obligations, going to church on Sunday, and not eating meat on Friday during Lent, will not help us to discover. We cannot simply do these things without exploring why we do these things. Is it because it's what our parents told us we should do? That's not enough.

The religious practices we engage in aren't just things that someone along the line decided would be nice to do. Rather, they grew out of a community of believers' collective experience of the spiritual life. Though the practice of religion can help us find our spiritual life, in a certain sense this gets things backward, even though the reality is that most of us get the religion first, and the spiritual life later. This is why so many people find themselves being "spiritual, but not religious." To advance in the spiritual life, and to find the life that God desires for each of us, the religion we have learned must in many ways be dispensed with in favor of a dynamic relationship with God which forces us to look critically at our past. Doing this many find (as I did, as Saint Ignatius did) that not only sin, but also rote religious practices, while good in themselves, can be an obstacle to allowing God to get through to us.

Twice in my adult life I wandered away from regular religious practice, not going to church every Sunday, not doing "churchy" things and in doing so I discovered a new adult religion. No longer was church on Sunday merely an obligation, something I was required to do. It now was something that grew out of my deepening relationship with God. I discovered that while I could be religious without being spiritual, as I often was as a child; as an adult I could not be spiritual without being religious. The more I came to appreciate my present, the more I was able to acknowledge my past, the more I was able to identify what God was calling me to in my experiences, gifts, and talents, the more I desired to be with God, not only in prayer, but in community at Mass, in social gatherings with fellow Christians, and on the streets with the poor. It is an essential experience of the adult spiritual life to move from the practice of the religion that was passed on to us to the living of a religion which rises out of the deepest desires of our heart. There's a great risk in this, we're bound to find ourselves lost for a time, but it's a crucial step in coming to be with God in the way that our hearts, and indeed God's heart, is restless for.

So, what have I been trying to accomplish in this first section of the book? I'm trying to say: You've got somethin' that none of us have. That's a wonderful, but also scary, reality. It means that you have to stop running away, and accept whatever Palookaville you find yourself in. It means you'll have to start chipping away at the scary bits of your life locked in the freezer of your soul, not just to deal with the bad things, but also to discover the good things that got stuck there with them. It means being OK with the fact that once you discover what that something is and begin to be what God wants you to be, there is no guarantee you'll be happy all the time, or even most of the time. It means coming to terms with certain ways you are special but, as I have been saying, that's true of all of us. So, this seemingly extraordinary reality that some of us would rather avoid is, in reality, one of the most ordinary realities of all.

Do you owe it to yourself to do all this? Well, yes, if you want to be true to who you really are and find the peace—and sometimes tur-moil—that comes with that. But more importantly, if I can step into the role of Chuckie again, you owe it to me, you owe it to other people, and you owe it to God who has made you for a purpose, one connected to that desire for God written in your heart which will grow stronger and stronger as you strip all this away.

I'm not saying this is an easy process. I'm not ignoring the fact that there are forces inside of you that will strongly resist. I know there are places in your past and even your present where you'd rather not go. I know you think you have plenty of time, and would rather wait to do all this later. The prophet Jeremiah was in much the same place when God called him. God came to Jeremiah and said: *You've got somethin' none of the rest have. I created you for a special purpose.* To which Jeremiah replied: *But what do I know about being a prophet? Who's going to listen to me?* Then, Jeremiah tells us:

> But the LORD said to me,
>   "Do not say, 'I am only a boy';
>   for you shall go to all to whom I send you,
>   and you shall speak whatever I command you.
>   Do not be afraid of them,
>   for I am with you . . ."

(Jeremiah 1:6–8)

That is God's promise to all of us. God doesn't just call us to risk ourselves in the purpose for which he created us, and then leave us alone. No, God promises to be with us, through the whole process. But often, given the mess we see when we look at our own lives, when we look out at the world and see all the evil that is there, we find ourselves asking, "Where could God possibly be in all this?" Let's go looking, because that's where we're going next.

CHAPTER FOUR

Who Told You That You Were Naked?

· · · · · · · · · · · · | *God Looks For Us Where We Are* | · · · · · · · · · · · ·

> But the LORD God called to the man, and asked him, "Where
> are you?" He said, "I heard the sound of you in the garden, and
> I was afraid, because I was naked; and I hid myself." He said,
> "Who told you that you were naked? Have you eaten from the
> tree of which I commanded you not to eat?" The man said,
> "The woman whom you gave to be with me—she gave me
> fruit from the tree, and I ate." Then the LORD God said to the
> woman, "What is this that you have done?" The woman said,
> "The serpent tricked me, and I ate."
> —Genesis 3:9–13

We've all had this nightmare—at least I have. I am back at school, junior high or high school. Everything's going along just fine until I realize I'm naked or wearing just my underwear and socks. I feel exposed, uncomfortable. It's a relief when I finally wake up and realize it was just a dream.

I suppose Freud might have something to say about the meaning of all this, some subconscious anxiety manifesting itself. Probably so. But I'm not as interested in that as I am in the fact that just about everybody seems to have had this dream, and most of us more than once. Here's something firmly lodged not just in the popular consciousness like a TV show, a song, or a movie. No, it seems to be lodged deeper in our collective *sub*conscious. I don't think anybody enjoys this dream. It seems we are all uncomfortable in one way or another with being exposed, with being naked.

This may sound kind of crazy, but I wonder if this dream might not be part of our spiritual inheritance as human beings, a vision that connects us with our original innocence, and original sin. It brings us back to the story of Adam and Eve in the opening pages of the Bible, the opening act of creation. It's the story of how the first human beings found themselves to be naked and, because of their sin, discovered the fear of being naked before God. Adam tells God: "I was afraid, because I was naked; and I hid myself." And God asks, "Who told you that you were naked?" This is an important question for all of us to answer because most of us, like Adam and Eve, are afraid of being naked before God. Like the dream which returns over and over again, we, because of our sinfulness, seem constantly subject to this fear. We are continually trying to "cover up" in our fear that God might come too close. We imagine—and we do the same in our relationships with other people—that if God sees us too close, and especially if God sees us *naked*, God won't love us and will want to punish us.

But think about God's question to Adam and Eve: "*Who* told you that you were naked?" It's not God who tells Adam and Eve—who tells *us*—that we should be ashamed of our nakedness, it's the serpent, Satan, the voice of evil that tries to get in the way of our relationship with God. The story of Adam and Eve and God's question imply that in our relationship with God we are meant to be exposed. That is the original innocence which God calls us to strive to return to, the place were we can unself-consciously stand naked with God. But to begin to do so we must acknowledge our sin and weakness, surrender our pride and that sense of having it "all together," of being healthy, of being normal. These are the things with which we clothe ourselves, that cause us to imagine that God is something other than our loving creator who would see us as ugly and be eager to punish us.

Because of this state of affairs, the confusion brought about by original sin and the voice of evil that tells us to be ashamed of our nakedness, sometimes the best thing that can happen to us is to find ourselves as we do in our dream, unavoidably exposed. This can happen in many ways. A wealthy entrepreneur suddenly loses everything. A celebrity is publicly humiliated. An addict hits rock bottom and can no longer deny her addiction. Or, as was my experience, a chronic illness can suddenly interrupt your life.

· · ·

It's kind of ironic that it first happened when I was helping lead a youth retreat. I got up in the morning, took a shower, and returned to my room to get dressed. And speaking of naked and exposed, I was only half-dressed when it hit me. I collapsed on the floor and started having convulsions, much to the shock of the person sharing my room, who kindly helped me to get fully dressed before the crowd formed. Then there were EMTs standing over me, asking me questions. Dazed, I didn't really know what to say, and *why was I lying on the floor, anyway?* I stood up and uncertainly let them lead me through the crowd of teenagers to the ambulance.

Later I learned that I'd had a seizure and, as it hadn't been brought on by any particular trauma, it was likely I'd have more. I could hardly comprehend what they were telling me. I was too young to have a disease. Could it be a mistake? What was God doing to me?

I made jokes to mask my anxiety. Since the name of the retreat I was working on was "Search," I couldn't resist. "Brings new meaning to the phrase 'search and seizure,'" I quipped. It didn't go over very well.

It was all very strange and confusing. The battery of tests they had performed read normal. They really couldn't pinpoint what was wrong with me, if anything. The most troubling news was that I would have to be put on anti-seizure medication, perhaps for the rest of my life.

Apparently they weren't exactly sure how it worked, just that it did. I was awash with uncertainty. Should I make myself dependent upon putting chemicals in my body every day? It wasn't the most compelling case. The medication they wanted me to take had side effects, yet I had no way of knowing if there was actually anything wrong with me, or if the medication would work. It may have all just been a freak, one-time occurrence. There was no way of telling, really. I wasn't really in favor of the idea of going on medication, and stubbornly resisted. It seemed a reasonable response at the time. The truth, however, was I just couldn't accept myself being so exposed—sick and dependent.

I took the medication for a time, then experimented a bit. I went for a two-year stretch being both seizure-free and medication-free. I imagined that I had my illness beat. Then came a wave of seizures—three in fairly quick succession. One forced me to expose my weakness to a professor when "out of it" after a seizure, I had to ask for an extension on an assignment. Another brought me close to serious injury when I whacked myself in the eye during a racquetball game. The scar above my eye remains, a symbol of my stubbornness, and also a reminder of how much worse things might have been had I not been wearing safety goggles.

•　•　•

With the help of a neurologist who liked to talk about classic literature and spoke of his powerlessness as a recovering alcoholic, I gave myself over to the need for medication. The irony had now become apparent that by taking the medication my illness was less likely to be exposed to others than if I were having seizures in public. And, remarkably, having accepted my illness and dependency, I became less and less concerned with the possibility that others might learn of it. I no longer felt the need to conceal my nakedness.

Still there was the question of why. I'd acknowledged where I was; now I wondered if God had a reason for putting me there. No matter how much I accepted it, I was still faced with the fear, fear that one day a seizure might come along that would cause serious, permanent damage to my brain. Much of what defined me could be lost in a second. Could God will that I suffer from this disease and this fear? That's a heady theological question to which there is not a simple answer. Put another way, you might ask: Can God bring about good by means of our illnesses, and even our fears? I am convinced God can—in this case, for two reasons.

·   ·   ·

The first is that once I finally accepted my illness and began to feel freer to talk about it, something interesting began to happen. Seemingly by chance, I would meet someone and somehow the conversation would turn to his or her struggles with epilepsy or seizures. It still happens— did just a couple weeks ago in fact. Where once I may have kept quiet, I find myself able to admit to them that I have suffered in much the same way. Suddenly, it's as if God has erased the distance between us and I am talking to an old friend—neither of us alone in our suffering. Having once known the loneliness of covering up the unwelcome nakedness of disease, I realize how important it is for me to enter into this moment, to be where I am, no matter the discomfort of exposing myself to this suddenly familiar stranger. God showed me in these moments how pain and confusion could be transformed into gift, if I let it. Once this finally sank in, I stopped asking God to take the disease away.

One of the most poignant of these encounters was with a woman named Carla. When I first met her, she was in pretty bad shape. Her seizures were not under control, and her doctors were still experimenting with various combinations of drugs to get her there. The result was that besides the anxiety of it all, the medication had her on a physical and emotional roller coaster. I found it easy to relate to Carla's situation, especially as she was about the same age that I was when I began having seizures. She was also being similarly stubborn in the face of the uncertainty of it all.

Because of our connection, she asked if she could see me for spiritual direction, and we began to meet once every few weeks. Though not exclusively, her condition was frequently the topic of conversation. At one point, as I had been, she was ready to give up on medication altogether, and take her chances. "When I have a headache, I take an aspirin," she argued, exasperated, "But here I am taking medication that makes me feel worse, when I feel fine!"

"I understand,." I said. "Every day it's the same for me. I don't feel bad, but I take my medication anyway. There are certain side effects that go with that, but they have abated over time. When it comes to this, you and I both have to treat this as if we *always* have a headache."

She understood, but she was still resistant, trying to come up with an excuse that made sense, trying to take control of things herself. I reached down deep into my experience and discovered the crucial question, one that ought to sound familiar to the one we began by discussing: "*Who* is telling you that you shouldn't take your medication?" I asked. "Is God telling you that?" That was the question that clinched it, for both of us. This was the question that I had failed to ask all those years ago when I faced similar frustrations. Both of us were afraid. Neither of us wanted to be weak, powerless, naked. But God wanted to break through all that, bring us face-to-face with where we were and ask: Who told you that you were naked? Who told you that being ill was something shameful? Who told you that sharing that illness with others was a sign of weakness? Who told you that doing the things that were necessary to stay healthy was to be powerless? This is not the voice of God.

There is also another gift that was given to me as a result of my illness. It is contained in two brief but important moments which I will never forget. The first took place during the ride home with my parents after that first trip to the hospital after the first seizure. In my memory

I see it as if I were witness to it, rather than a part of it. As we drove home, I started to feel as if I was going to be sick. We pulled the car over and I got out and bent over, convulsing with dry heaves. What I remember next is my father standing over me, holding me, as my body, along with the rest of me, tried to come to terms with the events of the day. And at the same time I could feel in a way I hadn't for many years at that point, my father's love for me, standing over me, protecting me, on the side of the road. I might live that day over again just for that moment.

It's a pity that for many sons and fathers, daughters and mothers, such moments are often few and far between. I would get one more such moment a few years later during my time of "experimenting." I was visiting my parents during a break from studies and woke up one morning to find my father embracing me tightly. The truth was, it turned out, that I hadn't just woken up. I had already gotten out of bed some time before and at some point in the course of the morning had suffered a seizure. So this waking up was not a waking up so much as coming back to consciousness after the seizure. "You scared the hell out of me," my father said, and through the fear I again knew that intense moment of the love of my own father which has helped me to see the love of my heavenly Father revealed in my experience of illness.

Such moments are important to remember, because the love of our parents is not always so immediate and obvious. For example, did you ever call home to your parents when, for whatever reason, you found yourself out past curfew? How did they respond? If your parents were anything like mine, the first words out of their mouths after "hello" would be—"Where are you?!" As the "guilty" party in this situation, whether I had a good excuse or not, whether they were meant that way or not, I took these words to be angry words. Indeed, I can remember one time that I was late because I had made the decision to help some-body who was stranded. I thought, "my mother will be proud of me." But after I explained everything to her, she still seemed just as angry.

According to the Bible, God's first question to the people he has created is "Where are you?" (Genesis 3:9) And, given the circumstances, it is easy for us to hear anger in this question. But, as with our parents, we easily mistake an expression of concern for one of anger. God, who, after all, created Adam and Eve out of his infinite love, is not angry, but concerned for the well-being of these special people. God's "Where are you?" echoes down through the centuries from the time when human beings first walked the earth to find each one of us where we are now. What do you hear? Anger? Concern? Love? How will you respond?

· · ·

God's question is one that most Jews, Christians, and many others are familiar with. It seems almost everyone knows the story of Adam and Eve. But, unfortunately, this beautiful story is rarely seen in a positive light. Most Bibles even entitle chapter three of Genesis, from which this passage is taken, "The Fall." It is true that Adam and Eve did something wrong. They broke a curfew of sorts, they did what God told them not to do. But what cannot be ignored in this passage is that when we fall, God comes looking for us.

An important step in the spiritual life is simply to answer God's question. God, who created you in love, who knows everything about you, is asking you, *Where are you?* This is not a question asked by an angry God. An angry God wouldn't care. It is important that we see this question for what it is. By asking such a question, God *is* out to expose you. Not so that he can show you everything that is wrong with you, or even everything that is right, but simply because God wants to be with you where you are, and whether we know it or not: God's *already there.*

This may be a bit hard to believe. Why does God care about me? In the introduction I spoke about our innate desire for God. We can come to know that desire by simply getting to know ourselves better. The harder thing for us to know, but just as important, is that there is a greater desire at work in our relationship with God—God's desire for us. We can have all sorts of images of God as a punisher, rule-maker, enforcer, all-powerful, and these get in the way of the simple truth that God's *Where are you?* communicates that God's greatest desire is to have a relationship with each one of us.

Nowhere is this passionate desire more evident than in the Old Testament. Unfortunately, we Christians often dismiss this part of the Bible as "old news." We can have the impression that once Christ came, none of that was important anymore. What's more, many of us find it hard to relate to God as he is found in the Old Testament. This portrayal can feed many of our worst images of God. God in the Old Testament is easily seen as nothing more than an angry, vengeful, and violent. But, as in the story of Adam and Eve, if we take another look we see a God who is more like a loving parent who acts out of great love for the people he calls his own. True, the relationship was a rocky one. God's people didn't always seem to want God's love, and God got angry, but he never stopped being with them. More importantly, he never stopped loving them.

Our relationships with God aren't all that different. They can be pretty rocky too. But another truth of the spiritual life we can learn from the Old Testament is that is precisely when things are rocky that we pay the most attention to our relationship with God. As neglectful as we may have been of our relationship when things were going well, God rejoices when we turn back to him. As all-powerful as God is, there is one thing he can never stop doing—loving us.

This is the same God Jesus is always pointing us toward, the one he calls "Father," and even more affectionately, "Abba." The Old Testament isn't old news, it's the first revelation of a tremendous love as real then, thousands of years ago, as it is today right where you are sitting.

. . .

When we begin to consider where we are in our relationship with God, it is important to be conscious of this sacred history. We find ourselves at a particular moment in the historical romance between God and humanity which began with creation and will continue long after this particular moment has passed. The truth we must take to heart as we begin this journey is that God loves us deeply and only wants what is best for each one of us. Jesus Christ is the ultimate expression of that love, as the Gospel of John tells us, and we are sometimes reminded by spectators at sporting events: "For God so loved the world that he gave his only Son, so that everyone who believes in him may not perish but may have eternal life" (John 3:16).

In the spiritual life, we cannot know where we are unless we have an awareness that God is somehow a part of wherever it is we find ourselves. When we stop to become conscious of where we are, we are challenged to ask: Could it be that I am where I am for a reason? Sometimes our lack of self-esteem, understandable in the early years of adulthood when everything seems so tentative and uncertain, prevents us from realizing our unique role in the divine romance. If I am in a good place, I might doubt that God could be so good to me. If I'm lost, I might be too busy finding my way or being frustrated with myself to see God's hand in my faltering. If I'm in a bad place, I might not be able to imagine God there at all or, if I can, I might wonder why God has chosen to punish me by allowing me to end up here.

So, sometimes answering the question, "Where are you?" isn't as simple as it might seem. The way we often live our lives—and see our lives—in any given moment is as a "between time." *Now* becomes defined as the time between where we are going and where we have been. Outside of that context, we frequently see the ordinary moments of our lives as having little significance of their own. Often this just isn't a limitation of our own view; frequently, this is how others see us. They only take notice when we do something significant, when we accomplish something, and, in some cases, only if that thing we do affects *them* in some way. Otherwise, it seems like they couldn't care less where we are. Because others measure our life moments in this way, we might begin to look at ourselves this way. We begin to wonder how much value our more idle moments have. When someone asks who we are, we point to past accomplishments or things we are looking forward to. We might ask: Isn't most of my life made up just of boring moments waiting for something to happen? Isn't that where I am most of the time?

If we are not to be in a constant state of restlessness, we have to find some way to come to an appreciation of where we are right now. This can be hard because it forces us to come to terms with the realization that we are unfinished, and to a certain extent will always be unfinished. In *The Holy Longing*, Ron Rolheiser paraphrased famous Jesuit theologian Karl Rahner, saying, "In the torment of the insufficiency of everything attainable we eventually realize that, here in this life, all symphonies remain unfinished."[1] Stop here, and slowly read that sentence again, because it's not so easy to get what he's saying the first time. "The torment of the insufficiency of everything attainable," what is that? Isn't it just a fancier way of describing that feeling I spoke of in the last paragraph? That wondering about the significance of the ordinary moments in our lives?

Now, consider Rahner's metaphor. An unfinished symphony is not something useless or unremarkable merely because it is unfinished. On the contrary, an unfinished symphony may contain movements, moments of harmony more beautiful than in any finished symphony. Indeed, if you've been to an art museum, perhaps you've seen an unfinished sculpture on display. If you avoided the temptation to pass it by simply because it was unfinished, you might have found it the most interesting piece in the entire museum. There, in a unique way, we have the mind of the artist right there before us! Our everyday moments can reveal things about the mind of the artist—God—that the high points and low points of our lives often cannot.

The challenge that comes with God's "Where are you?" is to see the beauty in the moments we often overlook in our rush to arrive at the next more interesting or pleasurable moments. The irony is that often during the moments we pay the most attention to, moments of great joy or great pain, moments of success or failure, we are far too distracted by all that is happening to see with the clarity that we can in our quieter and more ordinary moments. Yet, even our quieter moments can be filled with distractions.

As I sit quietly in my room, writing these words, some soft music playing, I am drawn by the unknown which exists outside my room. What are the other Jesuits that I live with doing? Is there a good movie on TV that I'm missing? Maybe I should invite some friends to go out tonight? I feel the pull of many other possibilities, all promising that they might be more fun than the exciting but solitary and tedious work of sitting in my room writing this book.

All of these things, however, would distract me from the beauty of where I am now. If I push these distractions aside, I look out my window and notice that the sun is setting, and the trees and the lawn have taken on that strange clarity that comes at dusk. A song has started playing which reminds me of the love of God: "You captured my heart," the singer proclaims. I am reminded that where I am now is the direct result of my own heart being captured by God's love, a "bondage" which moved me to choose to dedicate my life to God's service, and that moved me to write this book, so that I might share something of God's great love with you! Perhaps something I say might help God to capture your heart too, or remind you of how it has already been captured. I begin, then, to see where I really am, and suddenly things don't seem so boring anymore. Suddenly, the pull of those other distractions is not so strong. Suddenly, I'm present to God and to you in a deeper and more meaningful way.

Can you share this with me? Can you, where you are right now, contemplate the beauty of where you are? What do you see in your surroundings? What do you hear? Is there a song saying something to you? Are you sitting in silence? Are you hearing the unfinished symphony of everyday noise in the city or countryside? In these sights and sounds, in the words on this page, can you sense the presence of God? Can you hear the gentle voice asking: Where are you? Moving beyond your physical location and looking inside, what do you feel about your immediate situation? Are you happy or unhappy? Do you know the love of friends? Do you feel lonely? How are things in your family? Are you in a fulfilling relationship? Or are you in an abusive one? Has a significant relationship just ended? Are you ill? Are you experiencing the illness of someone close to you? Are you mourning the death of a loved one? Is this a hard time for you? Or have things rarely been better?

As you ponder these questions, try to avoid thinking what you might do about these things, how you might fix, change, or hold on to these feelings or experiences. Instead, just know yourself as the person who at this moment is defined in some way by these things. Accept yourself as this person, no matter how unresolved or uncomfortable things might be. Then, consider the one thing that remains constant where you are now, and no matter where you are. God is there with you in this garden of images and feelings, joys, and pains. God walks into that garden and invites you to consider the beauty of where you are, no matter the flowers that have not bloomed, or the weeds that have sprung up here and there. God is asking if he might share that garden with you. Will you let God be there with you? Not to judge you, not to make things worse for you, not even to make things better. No, God wants to be with you only because he loves you, exactly where you are—not because of anything you've done or not done in the past, not based on anything you might do in the future, but just because of who you are right now.

This is the meeting place of God's desire "only to be with you," and your desire "only to be with God." It is in such moments of quiet contemplation that we not only find God with us, but also find our true self. Though the complications of our lives impinge even on these moments, the feeling of peace which accompanies them reminds us that there is a nakedness before God of which we need not be ashamed. In love, God desires to be present with you no matter what your life is like outside these moments.

This would be a good moment to close the book and just pray in silence. The book's not going anywhere, and neither is God. Besides, God is the real expert on the spiritual life.

CHAPTER FIVE

The Cure for the Brain-Damaged Lucy

· · · · · · · · · | *Remembering God's Presence in Your Past* | · · · · · · · · ·

How long, O LORD? Will you forget me for ever?
How long will you hide your face from me?
—Psalm 13:1

When we've been given the gift of knowing God's presence in our lives in the here and now, it can be immensely comforting. It can bring a vibrancy to our life that seemed absent before. This was certainly the experience of Jesus' disciples. In the Bible, we are told how apostles like James and John literally dropped everything, seemingly without hesitation, to follow Jesus. They sensed that the arrival of Jesus in their lives signaled something extraordinary, something that was more important than anything else. And they remained with him until the end. James and John were working in the fishing boat with their father when Jesus called to them. Their Dad could not have been too happy when his two sons just dropped their nets and abandoned him in the middle of a workday! Or did he also recognize that with what his sons did God was doing something new?

Is God doing something new in you? Or are you still on the boat waiting for him to pass by? Each of us is uniquely gifted, and each of us uniquely complicated. Perhaps these chapters are in the wrong order for you. It is clear from the Gospel that not all the people Jesus encountered followed him as readily as James and John. The "sons of thunder," as the two were called, didn't need to see Jesus' resume, didn't need to know anything about him in order to follow him. Their nickname suggests that they were familiar with the unexpected and for them Jesus had a "thunder" which needed no introduction. But we are not all blessed with similar intuition, impulsiveness, and courage. In order to buy into the God thing, we need some evidence that God has already done something for us, that God has already been present in our lives.

• • •

When I was a little kid, whenever my siblings and I got a little whiny my parents would respond with something along the lines of, "I wish I was your age again, you don't know how easy you've got it!" Of course, I thought they were nuts! Who would want to be a powerless nine-year-old when you could have all the privileges that came with being an adult? Of course, I can see now something of what my parents were saying, but I still wouldn't want to be a kid again! Except, perhaps, for one reason: When I was in the single digit age range it was a lot easier for me to sense God's presence in my life. Now, you might say that this was just the power of a child's imagination. And, though I will talk about the importance of the imagination to the spiritual life later, I think it was more than that. It was a greater openness to the reality of God, uninhibited by "maturity" and the cumulative traumas that inhabit one's past as one grows older.

I think a lot of us would be better off in the quest to know God's love for us, and have a sense of his presence in our lives, if we were more easily able to return to a time of relatively unencumbered innocence. Jesus said that if we were to truly understand what he was all about, we would have to become like little children. Of course, it is impossible for us to become children again, but we can remember what it was like. And, it's interesting, I can't think of a major religious tradition in the world in which remembering is not somehow crucial to the way its members understand themselves and their relation to God. Indeed, for Christians, remembering is in many ways the center of our worship. The memorial acclamation or, as you might know it, the "mystery of faith," which we proclaim in the Catholic Mass, kind of sums it up.

· · ·

Without the remembering, our spiritual life, our relationship with God, is going to be a lot like the beginning of the movie *50 First Dates*. In it, the main character, Henry (played by Adam Sandler), meets Lucy (played by Drew Barrymore) and they hit it off. Indeed, Henry thinks he might have just met the girl of his dreams! However, when he meets up with Lucy again the next day, she doesn't know who he is! *This must be a joke*, Henry thinks, *how could she not remember him?!* Worse, it's not only that she doesn't remember him, but today she doesn't even seem to like him!

I expect, if we're honest, most of us can see that this is how we often treat God. God never abandons us. God is always eager to pick up where we left off in our relationship. But when we see God again, too often we can be like Lucy, not remembering who he is, and wishing he'd just go away. In the movie, we learn that it's not that Lucy is being mean. Rather, she has a brain injury which causes her to live the same day over and over again, each time she wakes up. For her, yesterday is always what she remembers about the day before her accident. She can't help that she doesn't remember Henry. When it comes to God's presence in our past, sometimes we seem to have a similar injury, and it's not that we hate God, sometimes it just seems that we can't help it either.

At first, Henry finds this an interesting challenge. Not unlike how God deals with us, each day he tries a different approach to making Lucy fall in love with him. Some days he succeeds. Other days he comically and even painfully fails. But after a while Henry finds that it's no longer just about the game of making Lucy fall in love with him. He realizes that he has fallen in love with Lucy. People discourage Henry, insisting that it would be too painful and difficult to have a relationship with Lucy, and a doctor assures him that there is no cure. But he will not be moved. He starts to keep a record of their relationship and their days together—he even makes a video—for her to review each morning when she wakes up, so that she'll know that this seeming stranger is no stranger at all. Lucy also starts to keep her own journal about their life together.

I think this is kind of the way that God approaches us. Not able to stop loving us, he gives in. God is willing to do whatever it will take to keep our relationship going, as long as we allow God to do it. To make his relationship with Lucy work, Henry realizes that every day he has to retell the story of their love and life together. It's a beautiful image of self-giving love and devotion. We, too, if we are to fully appreciate our relationship with God, also have to shore up our memories and constantly recall the way the God has been present—or sometimes not present—in our lives. And, as I hope I've illustrated, sometimes we'll be surprised by our forgetfulness, the times that we rejected God for something else—material gain, another person, our own egos—but, more importantly, we must also see the times in which, though we didn't realize it, God was already there.

In order to deepen our spiritual lives, then, we must all acknowledge that to one degree or another we are all like a bunch of brain-damaged Lucies in constant need of reminders of God's love for us. This is why we have to chip away at our past, not only to thaw our hearts, but also to put our new way of seeing to work, finding God there with us. At Christmas time, we sing, "O Come, O Come Emmanuel," which reminds us of one of Jesus' most important names. In Advent, the four weeks leading up to Christmas, this song is sung every week in some parish communities. It would certainly get my vote as one of the most over-sung Catholic hymns. But perhaps this isn't just due to a lack of creativity. Maybe it's because we know of our need to be reminded of what we all desire, deep down. *Emmanuel* means "God is with us." This wasn't just a fancy name for Jesus; Jesus was God's response to our desire to be with God, and a promise to all of us.

I won't pretend to tell you that if you look hard enough into your past you will see all the ways in which God was with you, even though you didn't recognize it. Many Christians will tell you that this is how you must feel, if you really have faith. But most of us know that as much as we would like that to be the case, it's just not that simple. There are painful moments in our lives in which to imagine God present would seem to imply that God is just an uncaring spectator. If God is good, if God was *there*, God couldn't possibly have just stood by as I was betrayed, beaten, or abused. To imagine God there would seem to make God an abuser too. Over the years, enough people have shared with me their stories of being abused that I know there is no simple answer that can account for the apparent inaction of God in those situations. But when we encounter the God who loves us at other moments of our lives, like the prayers of the psalms, like Jesus on the cross, we are at least moved to look back and say to the God of love: Why did you forget me? That's a prayer too, and a start.

Don't be afraid, either, to be angry with God. We've already seen with our look at some of the psalms, that not only does the Bible give us permission to be angry with God, but that God can take it! A stumbling block that many encounter when looking for God in their past is that they feel guilty, or even feel they've committed a sin, because they are angry with God.

I have had my own anger issues with God, about the story I'm about to tell you, and about the disease from which I suffer. I also know the anger that I've felt about people close to me who have been victims of abuse (how could God have allowed that to happen to them?) which I know can't even come close to the justifiable anger they might feel toward God. If you are a victim of abuse, or some other grave injustice, and you believe in a loving God, I can't imagine how you *wouldn't* feel some anger toward God, unless you've already managed to arrive at some healing and reconciliation. Not only would that not be sinful, but it would be pretty normal!

What I would suggest—as much as I hope this book might be helpful—that you not just read a book about it, but find someone you trust, maybe someone who has had a similar experience, and talk about it. Just that might be the beginning of a new relationship with God you might not have thought possible before. And, as I emphasized before, if you find the trauma is getting in the way of living a full and healthy life, and enjoying the love of friends and family, don't hesitate to seek some psychological counseling as well.

. . .

As much as I can look back and see the presence and action of God at many moments in my life, I find I still can not account for God's seeming inaction at a crucial moment in my life. I think just about everyone finds middle school to be a difficult time, but I had an especially difficult time getting through it.

I can confidently say that those years from sixth to eighth grade were the worst years of my life. Every day, it seemed, brought a new torture from bullies, my relationship with my father was going quickly downhill, and my self-esteem was falling even faster. My best friend stopped talking to me. I didn't know how to make things better at home. I found myself just feeling more and more alone. When you're that age, it seems like it might be this way forever. And who would want to live a life like that? God never seemed so absent from my life as he did then. I seriously considered taking my own life.

I still can't tell you what stopped me. Perhaps it was because I was the least violent person you could imagine; I even refused to fight back when someone tried to start a fight with me. And if I did finally try to defend myself I put so much energy into it that it was likely to reduce me to tears. My parents begged me to fight, but I never could see that as the right answer. Perhaps it was my cheerful disposition, which was both a blessing and a curse. It helped me to enjoy certain things in my life, and thus avoid falling too deep into despair, but it also masked how much I was really hurting. I'm not sure the people around me always realized how serious things were and, as is typical of that age, I didn't always want to talk about it.

I eventually wound up exasperated and, much like in the psalms of lament which I spoke of in the first chapter, I spoke my frustration. It had been a particularly trying day and once again I had been punched in the stomach for no reason but meanness. I arrived home and announced to my mother that I couldn't take it anymore. Perhaps she heard the exasperation in my voice, perhaps she sensed that I had reached the point where I might end it myself if no one else did, but that day she acted where before she hadn't. The week finished out, and when I returned home on Friday my mother told me the news: Despite the fact that it was the middle of the school year, on Monday I would begin at another school.

I still have a hard time looking back on that period of my life and imagining that God was there. Despite the reassurances of pious stories like "Footprints in the Sand," if I remember those days of getting picked on and beat up, I see no Jesus there with me, carrying me. The only way I can connect myself with Jesus at that time is to remember his words from the cross: *My God, my God, why have you forsaken me?* Even now, some thirty years later, while in faith I know that God was there somehow, if I identify with that twelve-year-old boy that I once was I find myself still asking, "God, did you forget me?"

And while that is still true, when I look back at that time, I also see something else. The day I arrived at the new school, which was in a neighboring town, I was introduced to Barry who, because he was from the same town as I, had been assigned to help me get adjusted. He was kind-hearted and welcoming, and fun to be around. We quickly became friends, which caused even our parents to wonder, because we were very different. Barry was good-looking, popular, athletic. I was none of those things, at least not in the eyes of most of my fellow students. Changing schools didn't change the fact that I didn't quite fit in. Yet, where others had abandoned my friendship for fear of becoming similarly unpopular, Barry seemed unfazed by such things.

This illustrates why facing the scary stuff from our past can be so important. I certainly didn't appreciate all this as it was happening. And I didn't even allow myself that opportunity when I was denying my past had nothing to do with my present. But once I had the courage to look for where God might have been with me during that time, I saw God's hand in my mother's intervention, and in the gift of one of the truest friends I've ever had. Though Barry and I have lost touch over the years, the memory of his friendship has only taken on greater importance as I've become more aware of the ways God was with me in my younger years, especially at the time God seemed most absent.

· · ·

This process, admittedly, also has another side to it. Some of us may suffer less from anger at what God allowed to happen to us than from shame at what we have done to God. In *50 First Dates*, Lucy and Henry's relationship seems to have defied the odds, as each day Henry dutifully shares with Lucy the story of their love for each other. But, one day, she overhears a conversation in which somebody mentions that Henry, a veterinarian at a local aquarium, has put on hold his dream to sail to the Arctic and study walruses. She, of course, realizes that he's done this because of his desire to stay and care for her. Assured by her doctor that her memory will never return, Lucy decides, in her love for Henry, that she doesn't want to be a burden to him in this way. Lucy breaks off the relationship, asking Henry to help her erase all memory of him, destroying the tape and all reference to him in her journals. Lucy also decides that she has been a burden to her family for too long as well, choosing to move to an institution for people with memory disorders. Henry, of course, is resistant, but reluctantly agrees.

Do we do a similar thing? Imagining that God needn't or shouldn't be burdened with us, do we look at our past as if God was never there, or only occasionally interested in what was happening? Sure, like Lucy does with Henry, we can choose to remove God from our past, or just fail to see him, but does that mean that God wasn't there? Just because we choose not to remember or acknowledge, does that mean that God wasn't with us?

In light of these questions, I think the end of *50 First Dates* is pretty instructive. (Spoiler Alert: If you want to see the movie and don't want to know the ending here—watch it before reading this next part). Henry sets sail on his dream journey, thankful, at least, that Lucy will never miss him. But then Henry turns the boat around and returns to Lucy, asking, "Do you know who I am?" "No," she says, but she asks if she can show him something. Lucy brings Henry to a studio, which is filled with her paintings, and though each one is different, each is unmistakably of Henry. "I don't know who you are, Henry...but I dream about you almost every night," she says.[1]

Henry and Lucy get married and sail together to the Arctic. And each day as Lucy wakes she is invited to watch a video which retells the story of Henry and Lucy's love and life together, and which also explains the child traveling with them!

Making progress in our relationship with God means letting God retell the story of our love and life together. God doesn't have to make a video or a mix tape to remind us; the tools we need are already available to us. The Bible tells the story of God's romance with the human race, and with each of us, over and over again. Our worship and regular participation in the sacraments also serve as reminders. And, most importantly, there is prayer. Making use of these other tools, we must prayerfully consider our past, remembering when God was there loving us, discovering those times that we failed to recognize God's loving presence, and trying to account for those chapters in our story when God appeared to be absent.

. . .

Besides being a burden to God, we may prefer to imagine that God wasn't there because we have been an embarrassment to God. Sometimes we have a hard time seeing God or Jesus in our past because we look at what we've done and where we've been and we can't possibly imagine that Jesus was there with us. Jesus would never go to that place, we think, and he certainly wouldn't hang around with *those* people who were doing *those* kinds of things. So, sometimes it's not that we find it hard to know Jesus was present because things were so bad, but because *we* were *that* bad. Now, I know that I may be being a bit presumptuous. Your life up to now might read like one of those perfect-from-childhood lives of the saints, and, if so, I think it is safe to assume you *might* be kidding yourself, because mine certainly hasn't been of one of those lives.

I needn't go into detail for you to imagine that I have been places and done things which I would be embarrassed to explain to Jesus (or my parents or my friends), if he were suddenly to appear. There were nights when I had a few too many drinks in college. There were the "harmless" pranks which no longer seemed so harmless when we considered the possible consequences. Most of us make poor judgments at times. Many of us are enticed into situations which are advertised to us as "fun," but which really turn out to be malicious, even evil. *Any chance, God*, we wonder, *that you could just erase that tape?* But, while we might be embarrassed to think that Jesus was there with us when we were doing our worst, at the same time it might reassure us that he will be there when we need him the most. Jesus' critics complained about him precisely because he gave his attention to those most in need—the ill, the disabled, *and* the sinners. In the Gospels, what made Jesus controversial was that he wasn't afraid to go anywhere or be with people where his help was needed. And his final words to the disciples in the Gospel of Matthew underline his intentions, "And remember, I am with you always, to the end of the age" (Matthew 28:20).

The point of all this is just to say that we have to be careful not to package Jesus too neatly in little boxes—*Jesus would never go there, Jesus would never be seen with those people*. Especially, because all too often *we* are those people being invited to find Jesus where we never thought he would be. Saint Augustine, at a crucial moment in his life, had a key insight into this problem. He realized that the desires he'd had in his life for things not good for him, and the pleasures he pursued, no matter how perverse, all had something of God in them. He reasoned that since God is the source of all good, and since the desire for God is something at the core of our being, anything that we thought to be good, even if we were mistaken in pursuing it, must have had something of God in it.

This is especially important because as you look back you might see times where Jesus *wasn't* where you thought he was. Sometimes we can mistake others for Jesus, and perhaps even more often we mistake our own egos for him. Usually this happens in that all-too-familiar process called *rationalization*.

So, here's a confession. I think we've all done things we regret, or will regret, if we allow ourselves to. Regret (for something we've done) is not such a bad thing, it reminds us that we're not perfect, and helps guard us against making the same mistake again. It also helps on the way to asking forgiveness, and allowing ourselves to be forgiven. There is little I would change about my life, because even when I think back to when times were the worst, I can usually see evidence of God's presence there.

This goes back to that time when I was in my charismaniac superhero mode. What had set me on that path was a powerful experience of God that I'd had the summer before at a charismatic prayer conference in Ohio. It was summertime, I had my Holy Spirit superhero T-shirt and I was psyched to head out to Ohio again. That was when my mom learned that she had blockages in her arteries which would require her to have angioplasty. Though there was some reason for concern, the surgery was a fairly routine one and was likely to go without a hitch. My dilemma came when the surgery was scheduled for the same time as the summer conference. My sister and I were already registered to go and, like I said, we were psyched. My parents asked us to stay home, but since we were adults (barely), the decision was left up to us.

I agonized over the decision, and turned to many for advice. *We could do more good for my mother praying with all those people than just staying here*, I convinced myself. The truth is that I didn't want to miss the conference and I was rationalizing. And I helped convince myself by dragging God into it. *Surely this is what God would want*, I thought to myself. Others in the group, enthused by the Holy Spirit as I was, were all too willing to support me in my self-deception. So, I went to Ohio while my mother went to surgery. Yes, I prayed, perhaps harder than I ever had. Still, it didn't take me long to figure out that this was clearly the wrong decision. God had nothing to do with it; it was all me.

Some months later, I had a shot at redemption. I'm not sure if I had yet realized how wrong I had been the first time, but I think I knew it deep down. My mother's first surgery hadn't completely taken, and they had to follow up with another of the same. This one was in some ways a little more serious, because if unsuccessful the second time, she would probably have had to have a more invasive open-heart procedure. This time, I did not fail to be there and, thankfully, another surgery was not required. I'm not so self-centered or morose to believe that this was God giving me another chance, but since this other chance had presented itself, I was going to make the most of it.

.   .   .

It's interesting for me to reflect on this episode in my life, because it probably was my first inkling of something which I now have come to take for granted—the importance of being present. We can all suffer from certain leaps of logic, like those I made when my mother had her first surgery. *What can I really do by being there? I can do more by going there and doing this.* We think, unless there is something concrete we can do, that our being there will be useless. But what I've learned by being with people when they were sick or dying, when they were grieving or in distress, is that though I can't do what I want to do, which is make everything better or say just the right thing, I can be there. At times, when appropriate, I can inject a little humor into the situation. At other times, I might just hold the person's hand, perhaps say a prayer. At other times, the person might not even seem to know I'm there, and I just sit with them a while, perhaps giving a family member a needed break.

At some point, I began to realize that among the many things I have the privilege of doing for people as a Jesuit and a priest, many of my greatest "successes" came when just "wasting time" with people. Often I find myself listening to people telling me their stories, all the while being frustrated by the fact that I can't do anything to help their situation. And I'm still surprised when, at the end, or maybe sometime later, they thank me for being so helpful. It might seem shocking that I would describe it as "wasting time," but I do so to make a point. We can get into the habit of measuring time in a consumer fashion, wanting to get our money's worth from the time we spend. But if we truly want to understand the importance of our presence in the lives of others, and their presence in ours, it will be helpful to look at things in terms of what we expect from God.

Though we should never completely let go of the expectation that God might directly intervene in our lives to make things better, we know that realistically this is not the way that things can or even should work. We must live with the mystery and the consequences of human freedom, which affect our lives in ways we cannot control, ways God could—but most often will not—overcome. The things we do, and the things that others do to or sometimes just around us, have consequences for our lives, good and bad. So, we learn to adjust our expectations of God just a bit. We want God to listen to us. We want God to be there for us. We also want God to change things, but this often will not happen immediately, though it might happen over time. But we also realize, for reasons known only to God, that change might not happen at all. In the Bible, for example, Saint Paul speaks of a thorn in his side which he asked God to remove three times, but God never did. Nevertheless, Paul had no doubt that God was there and had listened to his pleas. These are the ordinary expectations we have of God, though on occasion things might change without explanation, just so we remember that God can do that too.

There is something in our human nature, however, which will not let us be satisfied with just some abstract belief or sense that "God is everywhere." We need something more concrete. This is why belief in the real presence of Christ in the Eucharist has always been and continues to be so important in the Catholic faith. Daily, weekly, or sometimes just on Easter and Christmas, depending upon one's habits of worship, Catholics are reminded by receiving the bread and the wine, the Body and Blood of Christ at Mass, that Jesus is God-with-us. Jesus offers himself using ordinary matter, to remind us that God is in the substance of our lives. Because of that reminder, we must learn to see, then, as we look for God present in our lives, that often God's presence can only be seen in people like Henry, or my mother, or my friend Barry. It is in experiencing people "wasting" their time to listen to us, or just to be with us—which, translated, means to love us—that we realize more fully what "real presence" and "God-with-us" means. All of us have such experiences, though, like Lucy, we might be in need of frequent reminders. Eventually, though, when that memory of God with us is more fixed in our memory, even if sometimes in the back of our mind, we can confidently move forward, knowing that God will be with us in the future.

CHAPTER SIX

Stepping Out of the Boat
· · · · · · · · | *Will God Be With You Where You're Going?* | · · · · · · · · · ·

> Whether we call it restlessness, desire, or dis-ease, we all have
> a type of unrest that has the potential to drive us to God. Our
> vocation is about what we do with that unrest, that desire, that
> disease. We will be restless until we are living most fully the
> life that God calls us to live, and this will take a lifetime.
> —Renée LaReau, *Getting a Life:*
> *How to Find Your True Vocation*[1]

Even if you haven't spent much time reading the Bible, you probably
know the classic story of the young, ruddy shepherd boy David who
defeats the giant Philistine champion Goliath in battle. It's the classic
story of good triumphing over evil, against all odds. In contemporary
terms, you might say it's the classic story of "the little guy" sticking it to
"the man." It's another one of those stories that you can refer to and be
certain most people know what you are talking about. Even in everyday
language we often hear a daunting, seemingly insurmountable enemy
or institution referred to as a "Goliath." And, if that's the case, we hope
we are not on the other side, because we know that any "Goliath" is
going to be hard to overcome. So, just how did David manage to defeat
his Goliath?

I feel I should offer some kind of spoiler alert here, as the answer to that question is a little more complicated than the childhood versions of this story would have it. I was brought up to believe, more or less, that David's victory was something of a miracle, achieved because God was on his side. That last part is certainly true, but David's victory, perhaps, is not as much a miracle as we've been led to believe. And, as I hope you'll come to see, overcoming our youthful naiveté about this story is not necessarily a bad thing.

Certainly the fight was a mismatch physically. Goliath, whether he was a giant, or just unusually tall for the time, as many suggest, had a distinct advantage over an adolescent boy. But David wasn't without his advantages either. As he explains to King Saul when the king reacts skeptically to his offer to fight Goliath, as a shepherd David had rescued sheep from the jaws of lions and bears. *This boy had some skills.*

Saul reluctantly agrees, but encourages David to put on some armor, which turns out to be too heavy for someone of David's build. Still, David is undeterred. You see, David not only had some physical prowess and experience, but he was also a smart strategist. David wasn't going to go into a fight without a plan to win. The sling and stone he takes with him to face Goliath is often seen as the crude and ill-considered weapon of a young boy. Indeed, seeing David with such a weapon, Goliath is dismissive, and certainly not fearful. He thinks this is some kind of joke!

But think a bit more deeply about this scene and you'll see the brilliance in David's plan. First, the sling was not so crude and unconventional a weapon as we might be inclined to think. Armies of the time had entire battalions of slingers that marched into battle with them. Second, as we've already seen, it catches Goliath off guard and causes him to be overconfident. Finally, it shows that David wasn't just foolishly charging into a battle. He knew his weaknesses, what he could and could not achieve. One thing was clear: He could not defeat Goliath in close combat. But he could defeat him with an expertly-wielded sling and stone. And that is what he did.

So, when I read this story, it doesn't strike me as unbelievable or miraculous that David won this battle, at least in the same way it did when I was a child. What does impress me as unbelievable is that David seems to do it all without any fear. It's one thing to go up against Goliath and win, it's another to face Goliath and not even be afraid. David even seems to be motivated by a certain embarrassment at the fact that the army hasn't stepped up in this situation. He chides the men for letting their fear get in the way: "What shall be done for the man who kills this Philistine, and takes away the reproach from Israel? For who is this uncircumcised Philistine that he should defy the armies of the living God?" (1 Samuel 17:26). David's older brother tells him that he shouldn't say such things, but David challenges him to find something wrong in what he has said. For David, the bottom line is that the army should be confident, as he is, that God is on their side. If David was afraid, the writers of the book of Samuel chose to leave that part out. It seems very possible that he did enter into his battle with Goliath unafraid, unless he was putting up a very persuasive front.

•   •   •

I think perhaps why I find David's apparent lack of fear so unbelievable is that I'm so often fearful myself. This simply comes from being human. Fear is something that it seems we always have to contend with. And if it can infect an entire army, maybe we don't have so much reason to feel bad about its effects on us. But, often it paralyzes us, not allowing us to make progress in growing into the kind of person that God wants us to be, and that deep down we want to be, too.

Fear is a funny thing. We can overcome it in one instance, or over time, but it never seems to completely go away. My senior year of college I was given an unexpected and almost unbelievable opportunity which taught me a lot about the workings of fear. A fellowship was being offered which, if I received it, would give me the money to spend a year abroad engaged in a research project of my own devising. The application process was rather intense, but the fellowship itself only had a few basic requirements—I had to spend the entire year outside of the United States, was responsible for all arrangements including travel, living arrangements, research, and I had to give quarterly summaries of how the money was being spent, and finally, I had to write some kind of report on my findings. It seemed like the chance of a lifetime! I excitedly pursued it, with the support of friends and family, but also, sadly, with the fierce opposition of my girlfriend, Sarah. I wasn't exactly sensitive to her fears. Instead, I was angry at her lack of support, and the fact that she was treating the whole process like a rival. Plus, I was also trying to negotiate my own fears.

I went through the application process, outwardly confident, but inside preparing myself for failure. I was actually simultaneously driven by four fears. First, that I would fail. Second, that I would miss out on this opportunity. Third, that I might lose Sarah. (I wasn't clueless about her fears, just insensitive toward them and selfish about my concern for my own.) Finally, I feared that I would get it, but something would go wrong to prevent me from doing it.

When I did indeed receive the fellowship, the first two fears dropped away. Yet, the other two I carried with me until the day I had to leave. Once the plane was in the air, I no longer had to fear it not happening. Though that fear was still so immediate and strong that I can still remember the first dream I had in Sydney, my first stop. In the dream, I was in a panic, for somehow I had ended up back home in the United States, and I wondered how, with my limited financial resources, I was going to get back to Australia. It was a great relief when I woke from that dream to find myself still in Sydney. As for Sarah, we had a pleasant, if somewhat ambiguous, parting, and would stay in touch and even "together" despite the distance, for a time.

The fear, strangely, that I did not have was the most logical one. This was my first time leaving North America, and I was to do it for a year!

I was off to places I'd never been, having to find my way on my own. I did things that seem, in retrospect, kind of foolish. I entered into new situations ill-prepared, in ways I never would now, eighteen years later. I took risks and trusted people in situations in which my now more mature self would be much more wary. I'll never forget three days spent in Thailand during which I was preyed on by con men pretending to be friendly locals. I had coffee with one man who claimed to be a college professor. We had a pleasant conversation which, unfortunately, was punctuated by him trying to sell me gemstones that I knew to be worthless. I had been warned about this scam. So, as politely as I could, I told him I wasn't interested.

That same day, I met another man at a museum who claimed to be a tourist from the northern part of the country. He asked if he could join me walking through the museum. He seemed sincere. I even told him of my disappointment with my previous encounter! He bought me lunch, and then on the pretense of showing me something, tried to get me to enter into a jewelry store with him. When I refused to enter, he then tried to get me to lend him money! *Let me borrow some money to leave a donation at this temple*, he asked, *and then we can go to an ATM to get the money to pay you back*. At this point, I wasn't even going to take out my wallet, and I politely refused. He got pretty angry with me, but that was the end of it.

I decided I needed to get out of Bangkok, and booked passage to one of the islands. After a harrowing bus trip, we were dropped in the middle of nowhere and told to wait there for another bus. After a short while, some of the other passengers and I started to wonder if another bus was actually coming! Thankfully, it did. Once on the island, two friends I'd made on the trip down joined me in renting motorcycles. We toured the island, having to negotiate the challenge of driving on the left side of the road. At one point, I almost wiped out. Only then did I think of the possible difficulties I might face if I damaged the motorcycle.

Finally, sharing a cab to the airport with a couple I'd met on the train back to Bangkok, we asked the driver, whose little boy rode in the cab with us, if he could drop us somewhere to eat. He did, and offered to wait for us. So, while we were eating he waited in the car, with our luggage. He was still there when we finished eating. In retrospect, I was definitely foolish, and certainly not fearful enough. Several of these things could have turned out badly. But I also had a really good time, and the taxi driver's honesty made up for the dishonesty of the con men, and I learned that being a little less fearful, even if a little foolish, is not necessarily a bad thing.

I also had an experience in Australia which taught me something more about the nature of fear. I was there at a time when one of the popular things to do was to go bungee-jumping. I always said that was something I would never do. But then my friends and I found ourselves at the Great Barrier Reef. We experienced the beauty of the reef, went snorkeling, enjoyed the beaches and the night life there, and even had a brief scuba-diving experience. Then we went off to spend a few days in the nearby rain forest, where among the attractions was a bungee-jumping opportunity.

In a burst of enthusiasm one day, my friend Jerry and I decided to give it a try. But my fearlessness didn't last very long. This particular jump was not off a bridge, but off a crane. The bungee cord was tied around my ankles, and then I stepped onto a platform. That was easy enough. Next, the crane lifted the platform about three hundred feet into the air. That was when things got a bit scary. The bungee experts knew that, so I didn't go up in the platform alone. A member of the company's staff stood behind me on the platform. By the time the platform reached the top, my hands were pretty securely welded onto the railings. My companion said, "Don't look down, look straight ahead." I laughed, pointing out to him that I didn't need to look down to get a sense of how high up we were. "I don't think I can do this," I said. Even now, I get the chills just thinking about it.

I obviously wasn't the first person to say this, and he knew how to respond. After a bit of a pep talk, he asked me if I could let go of the railings and just hold my arms out to my side, resting them on his hands. "I promise not to push you," he added. He kept his promise. Then he instructed me not just to jump down, but to jump away from the platform, and, amazingly, I did. It didn't take long before the fear of falling rapidly toward earth was replaced by the exhilaration of being shot back upward as the cord tightened and responded. I'd done it. In truth, I should say *we* did it. It was my companion's reassuring and encouraging voice and presence that made the difference, even if, in the end, I was the only one doing the jumping.

I wish I could say that this cured me of the fear of ever doing this sort of thing again, but it didn't. Indeed, just days later this would be tested, not by another bungee-jump, but during a simple hike into the forest. In the midst of our hike, we discovered a pool of water surrounded by cliffs. This was an opportunity not only to refresh ourselves from our hike, but also to take advantage of the opportunity to jump from the cliffs which were, at most, fifty feet high into the water. But, when I climbed up to the edge of the cliff, I couldn't do it. I wasn't the only person asking the question: How could the man who had jumped from a height of three hundred feet just days before, not be able to jump from fifty feet into water? There was only one answer: fear.

. . .

One of my favorite stories in the Gospel also involves a jump into water. The Apostles are together in a boat on a lake one day, when they are caught up in a violent storm. As they struggle to right the boat and get to safety, they see a ghostlike figure coming at them across the water. Their anxiety about perishing in the storm is only heightened by this apparition. One of them cries out in fear, "It's a ghost!" It's not a ghost, but Jesus walking toward them on the water. He identifies himself and tells them, as he tells us over and over in the Gospels, "Don't be afraid." Well, you can imagine that worked about as well as the man on the bungee platform telling me, "Don't look down." How could they be sure it was Jesus coming at them through the storm? And, even if it was Jesus, how could they just suddenly not be afraid?

Peter, as if to test Jesus, then says something kind of crazy: "Lord, if it is you, tell me to come to you on the water." Jesus says, "Come." Peter, seemingly transformed from fear-filled to fearless (some might say foolish), immediately jumps out of the boat, and before he has a chance to think about what he's doing, begins walking on the water toward Jesus! Peter's fearlessness doesn't last long, however, for when he finally realizes that he's doing the impossible, he begins to sink under the water. He reaches toward Jesus and cries, "Lord, save me."

It seems Peter and David couldn't be any more different. David, confidently, fearlessly, and miraculously, slays the giant. Peter overcomes his fear temporarily, even to the point of walking on water, but becomes fearful again when he remembers that he can't do the impossible. David becomes a great hero. Peter manages to make a fool of himself.

Yet, despite this contrast, both these men become two of the most important figures in God's plan for his people. These two great biblical figures, and these two stories, need not be contrasted, but rather together can show us the way of finding our future with God. David's story teaches us the importance of self-knowledge. We cannot see what God is calling us to unless we are aware of the experiences and the talents which God has given us. As a shepherd, David knew that protecting his sheep was of paramount importance, even at the risk of his own life. Faced with a menace as daunting as Goliath, how much more important then, was the protection of God's chosen people? David was confident that God was on his side, and beside his experience, his analytical mind, and even his physical size seemed to make him the perfect man for the job, even if he was the only one that knew it.

Peter, on the other hand, was a fisherman. He knew very well he couldn't walk on water. He was quite familiar with his workplace! Self-knowledge, then, wasn't going to be of too much help in his situation. Peter was going to have to depend on his Jesus-knowledge. Unlike David, Peter is clearly very afraid. But he has also gotten to know Jesus well enough to be aware that when Jesus is around not only does he make miracles happen, but other people seem to be able to overcome both fear and their apparent limitations to do things they've never done before!

And the way the story ends tells us something else. Peter does step out of the boat. And, he does walk on water. *Briefly, at least.* But his flirtation with the miraculous is short-lived. It's not clear exactly why. Was he suddenly overtaken by fear? Or was it because he took his eyes off Jesus, as some say? Or was he distracted by the thought that what he was doing was beyond him? Whatever the answer, Peter soon finds himself sinking in the water. However, his struggle in the water was short-lived as well, because Peter instinctively knew what to do in such a situation. He cries out, "Lord, save me," and, as he knew he would, Jesus does just that. And, for us, this is, in many ways, the most important part of the story. It tells us that whether we are perfect for the job or just stepping out in faith, whether we succeed or fail, whether we are stymied by fear or apparently fearless, God wants to be there with us, and for us.

No matter how much we come to know about ourselves, and how strong our relationship with God becomes, we still face the reality that our future is uncertain. And, as strong as our faith is, we will never be free from fear, especially when our lives take an unexpected turn. But what we can learn from David and Peter's stories is that God will be with us in those situations in which our gifts and talents will more or less do the trick, God will be with us when we find ourselves doing more than we thought ourselves capable of, and often this is because God somehow makes up the difference. Most importantly, God will be with us when we fail. This last part is important. Peter's story shows us that even having found the faith to do the impossible is no guarantee against future failure.

• • •

A couple of years ago, I had one day in which I was a little bit David, a little bit Peter, and a whole lot *me*. I was doing a summer hospital chaplaincy internship program with about ten other people. Our days were a combination of group meetings and ministry to patients. About one night a week, we each worked an evening on-call shift, when one of us would be the only chaplain in the hospital. One Monday morning, during a meeting, we got an emergency call. One of the other people in my group volunteered to take it. When she returned, just a few minutes later, we wondered what was wrong. "They want a Catholic," she said. All eyes turned to me—I was the only Catholic in the group. So, off we went, together.

I introduced myself to the family, explained that I was a Catholic seminarian and summer chaplain. They introduced me to the patient, a husband and father, who had had an unexpected stroke that morning. I was ready to do whatever was necessary to help these people out. We started with a "Catholic" prayer, and then the other chaplain and I set about seeing what else we could do. Did they want to talk? We lingered. They said very little. It became awkward. I soon realized that they just wanted someone to come, say the prayer, and go. We eventually extricated ourselves, but not without feeling that we had messed up somehow. I found myself becoming almost resentful. *That's it?* I thought. *Why insist on having a Catholic chaplain, when all you wanted was a prayer? The other chaplain would probably have said a nicer prayer than I did!* I feared that by causing such an awkward moment, instead of helping, I might have made things worse.

The day continued, and at some point in the course of it I realized, to my horror, that I had made another mistake. I was not on call the next night, as I had thought, but that same night. I hadn't had the opportunity to prepare myself. My mind was scattered, not rested or calm. Nevertheless, I stayed for my shift. My first visit was to intensive care. "The patient in room number five just expired," the desk nurse informed me. "The family is there. Maybe you could say a prayer with them." *Is this really how I'm going to start my night?* I thought. I pulled back the curtain to find about eight family members crying, embracing one another, surrounding the bed of the dead man lying there. I felt like an intruder. But there was no turning back. I offered to pray. I asked his name. "David." Instinctively, I put my hand on his arm. I prayed for David, and for the people gathered there, lingered in silence briefly, and then explained that if I could do anything more for them, to ask the nurse to call me. They thanked me. I left, wondering: Did I leave too quickly, because of what happened in the morning? More so I wondered: How did I know to touch his arm? And why didn't it scare me?

I moved from there into "regular" visits. I spent some time with a teenage girl who had been experiencing seizures. I talked with a patient who was a doctor who asked not that I pray for him, but merely think good thoughts about him. During the course of these visits, my pager went off twice.

The first page came while I was telling the young woman about my own experience with seizures. I returned to intensive care where three daughters were attending to their father, who had not been given long to live. They introduced me to the patient, and I said hello, though he was not conscious. *Just a few days ago he had been playing with his grandson,* they said. A priest was coming to offer the sacrament of the sick. I waited with them. I learned much about them and their family in that short time. Their brother arrived, regarding me with some suspicion. Eventually, the priest arrived. I prayed with them as the priest anointed their father. Sensing that was enough, I said good-bye to each of them, telling them to call for me again, if needed.

I'd hoped that would be the last end-of-life visit for the day. I'd already had more than the usual share. But as I was chatting with the "good thoughts" doctor, the pager rang again. This time it was from the ER. I arrived to find that a young man had shot himself in the head. I was afraid, for a moment, they expected me to go into the trauma room with him. I wasn't sure if I'd be able to handle that. But what they needed from me, the nurse explained, was to wait for the family. They knew that the family, whoever they were, would be coming. But, since the young man had come in without any identification, they didn't know who or when or how many. "How will I know who they are?" I asked. "You'll know them when you see them," she insisted.

They were very long in coming. After quite a bit of time, a couple walked in. As the nurse had predicted, I knew immediately it was them, I could see it in their faces. I greeted the man's parents. And though we were supposed to go to the family room, the nurse intercepted me and asked that we come straight to the ER. On the way, the mother opened her hand, revealing her rosary beads. "Good thing to have," I said. She nodded solemnly. I stood by them as the doctor told them that their son's chances were not good and given the nature of his injuries, it would probably be better that he not survive. They reacted calmly; this seemed to be what they expected. When the doctor asked if they wanted to see their son, they said no. They said they would see him later —at the hospital he would be transferred to.

I led them back to the family room. On the way, the father asked if I would see to it that his son receive the anointing of the sick. I told him I would do my best. A friend of theirs joined us in the family room. I said a prayer. They thanked me, the mother hugged me, and they were gone. I was spent. I went back to the chaplain's office to finish the night's paperwork. I had no energy left for more visits.

I called the on-call chaplain at the other hospital to make good on my promise to the father. The priest on the other end of the line, apparently not fully understanding the circumstances I had tried to explain, snapped, "Why didn't you do it there?!" After the night I'd had, I was tempted to a less-than-charitable response. But remembering that this was about honoring the father's request, and that such a response might get in the way of that, I simply tried to reiterate that point and thanked him. Before I went home, I called Abby, the chaplain with whom I had started the day. I knew I couldn't just drive home—it was about a forty-minute drive—carrying the weight of this, I needed to talk to someone who would understand.

As you might imagine, I did and have spent a lot of time reflecting on that day. Though I had experienced some similar situations in the past, I had not encountered precisely the types of situations I had that day, and certainly not all at once. Even in the instances where I had doubts about whether I had gotten things right, I was amazed at my calm, and sometimes the fact that I knew what to do at all.

The answer was a combination of the formation and experiences which I'd had in my priestly training, which, like David's experience as a shepherd, had instilled certain instincts and skills in me, and a surrendering to the grace of God which, as in the case of Peter, allowed me to do more than I alone was capable of. Though I will never be free from fear or failure, as that day also proved, I realized that I was at my best the more I was able to get myself out of the way. I saw this illustrated in my frustration that morning. It was really a result of the fact that *I*, especially because I was "the Catholic," wanted to do more for them, and they weren't allowing me to. I wasn't content to simply be what they needed me to be at that moment. I had to remember, as I did when I held my temper with the priest at the end of that night, that it was about them, and not me.

A year later, I was brought back to that day in a surprising way. The writer Joan Didion had been receiving accolades and rave reviews for her latest book, *The Year of Magical Thinking*, and so I had placed it on my summer reading list. It's a powerful and deeply moving account of her experience of her husband's death and the year that followed. I found myself grateful for all the things the book said about love and grief and, in a strictly personal way, what it didn't say. She barely describes one encounter with a priest, in the hospital on the evening of her husband's death: "They asked if I wanted a priest. I said yes. A priest appeared and said the words. I thanked him."[2] At first, I found myself asking, *why did she even bother to mention this priest, when it seems like he didn't really help her?* Then it struck me. Joan Didion is not a writer who wastes words on insignificant details. If she mentioned this encounter with the priest, it was important to her, even if he just "said the words." Maybe that priest felt like I did that Monday morning, or maybe he already knew what I've since discovered, that when God's involved, just being there for a moment and offering words of comfort and prayer is not necessarily that far removed from slaying giants and walking on water. We just need to take the focus off ourselves and let God work.

●　　●　　●

Because God works in us in such simple and dramatic ways, we can be confident that God is with us. Not just because God is omnipresent, but because God loves each one of us and has a future in mind for us which will fulfill our greatest desires, even if we don't really know what they are yet. Our task, and it is not always an easy one, is to start living into that future. And that means making the needed changes to be the person that future requires. Just because God loves us as we are, doesn't mean that God's OK with us staying the same.

When I told a friend that I thought God was calling me to be a priest, and that I was joining the Jesuits to see if I was right (even though I was fairly certain), she asked, "Does that mean you don't want to get married and have children?" I think she was a little surprised when I said, "No. I would love to be married and have children. But I don't think that is part of what God wants for me. Right now, my greatest desire is to do what God is calling me to do. If that means being a priest, then that also means marriage and children are something I'll be required to give up." Though this is not true for every man called to be a priest—some know they are not made for marriage and children—this still continues to be true of me. Our sensibilities struggle against this, especially those of us formed by American culture. If you have a desire for both, we think, you should be able to do both.

Maybe God wants you to be an Episcopal priest, some might suggest, then you could be a priest *and* be married. But in my case, I have become convinced that not only is God's desire that I be a Catholic priest, but also that I be a Jesuit priest. And no matter how people may joke sometimes, you can only be a Jesuit if you are Catholic.

This also precludes another option that people sometimes think I might choose. People often say to me, "If the Church let priests get married, you'd get married, right?" Then I have to explain to them that if that were to happen, that would only apply to the diocesan priests, the priests that work directly for the local bishop, and not for those of us who belong to religious communities. Marriage would still not be an option for us, because our way of life, living in community, and having always to be ready to answer a ministerial need, to even move across the country or the world at a moment's notice, would not allow for it. The wife and kids might not be too happy learning that the Jesuit Father General has asked that we move to a poor village across the world, and that we are leaving tomorrow!

The truth is, as I have already suggested elsewhere, is that even if we ignore what God wants, we can't have all that we want. We might end up getting much of what we want, or very little. The difference that comes from paying attention to what God desires is that we eventually find that what we want, and even the way in which we want things, changes. We develop a great desire—though this, unfortunately, doesn't mean other desires won't get in the way from time to time—to grow into God's desire for us, for *me*.

One of the ways which Saint Ignatius of Loyola advised for doing this was to become what he described as *indifferent*. This has to be explained carefully these days, because the word *indifferent* has come to mean, basically, "I don't care." Which is not what Ignatius meant. For him, it is a result of caring *a lot*, about God's will, and about others. He summed this up in what he called "The First Principle and Foundation" of the spiritual life:

The human person is created to praise, reverence, and serve God Our Lord, and by doing so, to save his or her soul. All other things on the face of the earth are created for human beings in order to help them pursue the end for which they are created. It follows from this that one must use other created things, in so far as they help towards one's end, and free oneself from them, in so far as they are obstacles to one's end. To do this, we need to make ourselves indifferent to all created things, provided the matter is subject to our free choice and there is no other prohibition. Thus, as far as we are concerned, we should not want health more than illness, wealth more than poverty, fame more than disgrace, a long life more than a short one, and similarly for all the rest, but we should desire and choose only what helps us more towards the end for which we are created.[3]

I remember that when I first encountered these words in the novitiate, I was a little bit put off. It seemed to be saying that the thing I should care about most was my own salvation, and that I should see things—and people!—in terms of whether they were of use in helping me achieve that goal. If not, *get rid of them!* Certainly, I think this is a case where Ignatius' more practical side sort of trumped his human instincts, and he didn't put things as delicately as he might have. And what is not made as clear as it could be is that this is not simply an individual thing. Our salvation is not ours alone, divorced from community. We are saved *with* others. So this does not mean to cast off everyone who gets in the way of my easy road to salvation. But it does mean challenging others, like Chuckie did for Will in *Good Will Hunting*, to pay attention to God's will for their lives. Once we start doing that, the truth is that some people will resent us for it, and we will lose their friendship. Chuckie is willing to let Will become somebody else for Will's own good, but not all of our friends turn out to be so selfless. They don't want to be saved with us. Because of that, we have to let them go to find another way.

But the basic idea is this: Pay attention. It means examining our lives to see which things—and people—in it are helping us to grow in our life with God, and understanding of God's will, and which are not. There are some people who will never let you be more than the person they used to know. They will not accept the "new you." And, if that's the case, unless you can somehow convince them to knock it off, they will be a constant drag on you, tempting you back to a life God has called you out of. They want you to stay in the boat, and God's telling you that you've got to step out!

This is not to be taken lightly. Later, I will talk about how important friendship is for the spiritual life. The idea of the holy person, separated from everything but God, is not really a Christian vision of things. The Bible is not the story of God's relationship with a bunch of individual people; it's the account of his love affair with a community of people, and ultimately all of humankind! It's hard to lose friends because we are not made to be alone, or to be saved alone. This becomes clearer when we realize how God is present, not just in other people, but in so much of what we experience. Living according to God's desire calls upon us to see God more and more in our daily lives, to do so as part of community and, like David, Peter, and all the apostles, to choose to act on the holy desires this nurtures inside of us.

CHAPTER SEVEN

What's So Amazing That Keeps Us Stargazing?

· · · · · · · | *Contemplative Prayer and Contemplative Living* | · · · · · · ·

The rainbow never tells me
That gust and storm are by,
Yet is she more convincing
Than Philosophy.

> —Emily Dickinson[1]

There are certain things in this life that we never seem to grow tired of. Rainbows. Fireworks. A star-filled sky. What is it about these things that no matter how many times we've seen them, no matter how many times in our busyness we have passed them by, they never lose their capacity to fascinate us, when we take the time to indulge ourselves in them? We grow accustomed, and even bored, of so many things in our lives—that thing we just *had* to have quickly no longer holds any wonder for us. Fresh novelties take their place, and we may turn back to them now and then for the sake of nostalgia, but we'd rather have the latest thing. But how might our lives be different if the everyday things we take for granted, as well as the new things, never lost their capacity to fascinate us, always had the potential to excite our wonder? Is this even possible?

I'd like to be able to tell you that once you've found your place with God, that your life would be transformed in this way. Every moment would be a moment of holy wonder. But I can't. Is it possible? Yes, I think so. Is it automatic? Absolutely not. It's something you have to work at. Not only that, it's something you have to stick with. For me, that means I already have at least one strike against me. I can gather up the enthusiasm to work at it, for a time. But stick with it? Forget it. My mind hardly slows down enough to allow me to speak sometimes. Contemplate the universe? That's something I'm never completely going to be able to make a go at. But what's comforting, after having done some of the work of the preceding chapters, is that I know this, and I know God knows this. If you've made it this far in the book, and you can stop to think for a moment, I'm guessing you can find a similar comfort in wherever you are.

• • •

The great amphibian philosopher Kermit the Frog once sang the question, "Why are there so many songs about rainbows?" Now, honestly, I can only think of about two songs about rainbows, but still Kermit's song came to mind as I began my annual eight-day silent retreat a couple of years ago. The first day of the retreat, there it was, hovering over the retreat house—a rainbow. One of the great things about being on a silent retreat is that you have no choice but to pay attention. So, with Kermit's voice echoing in the back of my mind, I started to think about rainbows.

Though Kermit would likely disagree, the first thing I thought was that rainbows are kind of boring. Really, think about it. They're the same, *every* time! Red-Orange-Yellow-Green-Blue-Indigo-Violet, the colors never change. Wouldn't it be more interesting if, just once in a while, the order got switched around a little? How about green next to red? Or yellow next to, say, indigo? Maybe get rid of a color. Kermit also once said, "It ain't easy being green," so how about we lose the green? Or add a color—magenta might be nice.

Then I thought: *Mark, that's just your problem. You can't just be content to let things be the way they are. Who are you, anyway, to rearrange the order in which God created things? Maybe God doesn't like magenta. And maybe God knows just a little bit more than you about putting together a universe.* That's what *I* was thinking, anyway.

But, then, as I was still busy beating myself up, something else occurred to me. I thought, *wait a minute.* Maybe the fact that it's the same every time isn't boring at all, but actually kind of cool! God has given us something we can count on! After all, what is it? It's just light refracted through moisture in the air. In a sense, there is nothing there that wasn't there before. We tend to see rainbows as an uncommon phenomenon, but in a real sense they are simply a manifestation of one of the things in our lives we take most for granted—light. Isn't it interesting that in our faith tradition one of the symbols we use for God and Jesus is light? This, of course, is a reminder of how God illuminates things and dispels the darkness, but it can also serve as a caution to us that as we do with light, we might have a tendency to take God's presence for granted as well. That is, until there's a blackout, until something dramatic happens, good or bad.

Depending on where you are in your life, you might react to this in one of two ways. You might feel a little guilty for having taken God for granted. Or, you might feel comforted by the thought that, like light, God is always there, even if it's been a while since you've seen a rainbow. Come to think of it, you probably feel a little bit of both. That's how I feel most of the time.

Well, back to that rainbow on my retreat. In the end, I was thinking more or less along the lines with which I started this chapter. Isn't it great that however mundane the world can seem sometimes, there are these occasional things that always hold a certain fascination for us? Rainbows and whatever fascinations are unique to you are reminders to be attentive to the things we take for granted and the everyday fascinations they might hold. Among the things this kind of reflection has taught me is that God has a perverse sense humor. So, I wasn't totally surprised when looking out a window later that night I saw a single firework rise up into the air and explode over the landscape behind the retreat house. *Yeah, I thought, that's God messing with me again.*

Now the point here hasn't really been to answer Kermit's question or sing the praises of rainbows. The point is that what I just described wasn't just the random thoughts of a crazy Jesuit (despite what you were thinking), but prayer. Remember what I said about how a silent retreat forces one to pay attention. That's half the battle with prayer, giving it your attention. But this points to something that I think can actually get in the way of prayer. Many of us were brought up to think that unless you're reciting the Our Father or the Hail Mary, the rosary, or something like that, you aren't really praying. Those are wonderful ways to pray that we should always have in our prayer tool kit. But we also need time to pay attention, to just be quiet and let God speak to us. Chances are, though, God is not going to speak to you with an audible voice. That is why contemplation of nature, of an icon, a piece of artwork, or even a song can come in handy. It helps to focus our attention. Notice that as all over the place as my prayer might have been, it kept coming back to what I was focusing my attention on—the rainbow, and God. And how did this happen? By letting God speak to me by means of my imagination.

One of the greatest insights Saint Ignatius of Loyola had was about how powerfully God could speak to us by means of our imagination. Remember that an important element of his conversion was imagining himself doing the kind of things that Saint Francis and Saint Dominic had done. One of the most important things for me in my discernment about becoming a priest was to come to the point where I could actually imagine myself being a priest. I assure you *that* was no easy task! It's unfortunate that the imagination sometimes gets a bad rap. We uses phrases like, "It was just my imagination" to discount experiences that are unusual or that we don't understand, presuming that they couldn't have been real. Or, we can see our imagination as a distraction and shut it down every time it starts to go to work. In this way, the world does indeed become very mundane because we get in the habit of only seeing what's right in front of us, failing to discover the deeper meaning and significance which the experiences of our lives, and our prayer, can hold. If we want to better find meaning in our lives, and get more out of our contemplation and prayer, we need to heed the advice which we've all probably been given at one time or another in our lives: Use your imagination!

. . .

I used to teach poetry, and students would often get frustrated with it. They often saw poetry as a puzzle. More than one complained to me about the difficulty of finding the "hidden meaning" in each poem. Frequently, they found it difficult to get beyond the literal meaning of the text without throwing their hands up in despair and saying, "it could mean anything" or, they would insist, that there was no right interpretation. Thus, the argument continued, I couldn't give them a grade because it meant whatever they interpreted it to mean. They didn't get very far with this argument. It's true that a poem can have multiple meanings, but there are meanings that it *can* have and meanings that it *can't*.

Prayer can be much the same way. There are definitely many things that God could be saying to us, but there are also clearly things that God would not say to us. That's why I've encouraged you as best as possible to get a sense of where you and God are in relation to each other. These are the parameters in which God will speak to you. So, for example, you can be certain that God would not ask you to do something that both you and God know would get in the way of your relationship, or your well-being. If you're an alcoholic, God is not going to tell you that your mission in life is to be a beer-taster, or a wine connoisseur. This is where having a spiritual director helps. When you think God is saying something to you, but you're unsure, your spiritual director, who knows your relationship with God can ask: Who told you that? Are you sure it was God?

This is why some people fear the use of imagination in prayer. How, they ask, do I know that God and not the evil spirit is speaking to me; or how can I tell if it's not just me talking to myself, telling myself what I want to hear? These are important questions that must be answered, but we should not let them prevent us from opening ourselves to God in this very powerful way. We should be willing to take the risk, trusting that God won't let us misinterpret things too badly if we have sufficient self-knowledge and trust in God's love.

Few things illustrate this intersection between contemplation and imagination better than poetry. The poet has to have the confidence that what he or she sees is not totally random, the poetic vision is at work here, not only seeing things in a different way, but also seeing things in a way others will be able to see too. Otherwise, the poem would make sense only to the poet. And then it might just be a sign of mental illness. Similarly, we have to trust that the prayer part of each one of us, which all of us have because God created us, will help us to see God in the various ways in which we experience the world— whether in nature, events, or other people. God has gifted us with certain individuals in whom both these sensibilities were strongly at work. One of these people was Gerard Manley Hopkins.

Gerard Manley Hopkins was a Jesuit priest who lived in the nineteenth century, and who became a famous poet. To me, he serves as a good example of a person who exemplifies the fact that living God's will for one's life is no guarantee of happiness. Indeed, many agree that Hopkins's life may have been happier had he not chosen to be a Jesuit and a priest. He was prone to depression, found it hard to live with others, and others found it hard to live with him. Yet, had he not chosen to live that life, and to endure its challenges, he may not have produced some of the most profound contemplative poetry ever written. His life as a Jesuit and a priest afforded him the opportunity to bring together his faith, attention to the world, and his imagination in remarkable ways. Consider one of his most well-known poems, "As Kingfishers Catch Fire." It begins with mentioning everyday things—the flight of a kingfisher, a large bird, the smaller but still dramatic flights of dragonflies, the sound of a stone thrown into a well, the notes produced by the strings of a musical instrument, and the "voice" of a church bell. Hopkins shows us where the contemplation of such simple things can lead us as we think about them in light of our relationship to God. The beauty and the music produced by these things speak to us of God, and invite us to contemplate how each of us in our ordinariness does the same. They also speak to us about vocation, how each element of nature witnesses to God in fulfilling its purpose, the purpose given it by the Creator. As we contemplate these things, Hopkins suggests, we can begin to get in touch with our own unique vocations, "speaking" and "spelling," and "Crying *What I do is me: for that I came.*"[2] Indeed, he goes on to say that we act who we are. That as a bell has no choice but to ring, so we, if we are "just," for example, have no choice but "justice" (that is, to do what is just). In becoming the person God has created us to be, we, according to our vision of faith, show Christ to the world.

Wow. We started with a bird, an insect, and a church bell, and look where we ended up! Here, again, though the connections may seem somewhat random, in the hands of a poet like Hopkins they become a deep and most profound prayer. The message that Hopkins and many of the greatest poets hold for us is that deliberate and prayerful attentiveness—what is, in religious terms, often referred to as contemplation—reveals to us the beauty and the wonder of the everyday, and this by allowing our mind, our heart, and our spirit to make connections we may not have otherwise thought to make. *Why are there so many songs about rainbows?* Because there are at least as many things to say about rainbows as there are people to see them.

Now if nineteenth-century poetry is a bit much for you, why not look to contemporary pop music for inspiration? Sure, there are those music artists who are just out to make a buck, and who may be a bit lacking in spiritual depth. But I make a habit of seeking out songs and artists that speak to me in meaningful and spiritual ways. Some are poets in their own right like Bruce Springsteen, U2, Sarah McLachlan, Paula Cole, Jewel, Coldplay, Madonna, Dave Matthews, and many more. Now, I'm not saying they all live exemplary lives, neither did many of the greatest poets, but there is a depth to their work worthy of taking notice of, even if we might not choose to imitate their lifestyle.

Despite her early "bad girl" image, one artist whose work I have found particularly intriguing over the years is Alanis Morissette. Many of her songs reveal a depth of contemplation not unlike that of a Hopkins. She has a song in which she looks at her past life and takes the time to be grateful for the gifts she has been given in the experiences that she has had, but also in that spirit of gratitude examines things that might need changing in her life. It's called "Thank U." In it she questions some of the things in her life, and follows these questions with a chorus of thanksgiving.

One of the things that is likely to strike you about this song is that the things she is thankful for are not exactly the kind of things you would expect. Terror? Disillusionment? Frailty? What's she talking about? Who's thankful for that?! Yet, this was a hit song. And I bet it caused many to ask the same questions. You may remember having done so back when radio stations were playing it ten times a day! I do.

Morissette brings us here to a couple more important insights about living and praying in a contemplative way. The first is that it's not just rainbows, star-filled skies, or a child's laugh that reveal God to us. Sometimes God is revealed most powerfully in our lives by bad things that happen, by ugly things. Twice in my life I've been fired from a job. Once a long time ago, but the second time fairly recently. I can assure you that neither time I felt good about it, or saw much of God in what was happening to me. But I can look back now and see that in both instances that if God's hand wasn't in it, God certainly made the most of it, because important and life-transforming new doors were opened to me as a result. Similarly, I would rather have not been living in New York City when the September 11 attacks occurred. Being so close to that tragedy threw me into a deep funk that I was only slowly able to come out of. But when I did, God used the opportunity to unveil a whole new aspect of his will for me, challenging me to take my convictions about peace and justice much more seriously. So, when Morissette thanks *terror*, I don't think she's saying that she likes the feeling, but rather that it helped her wake up to something. Part of living contemplatively is being open to both the awful and wonderful ways God makes himself known in our lives and to respond in prayer.

The other thing Morissette demonstrates for us is that once one realizes this contemplative attitude, one finds reason to be thankful. In chapter five I spoke about how our worship has so much to do with remembering. It also has everything to do with being thankful. The word *Eucharist* which, in the Catholic tradition, we often use as a synonym for worship, means "thanksgiving." Contemplative living is kind of like worshipping on the move. We see and remember how God has been revealed to us in our everyday experience, and we give thanks. "Thank you" is one of the shortest and most important of Christian prayers. Another, even shorter one, is "help." The contemplative life should also remind us that God is there to help us.

This talk of contemplation might very well bring you back to chapter four's invitation to contemplate how God is present to you in your life right now, and you should by now have a better understanding of how God is present in your life. "Contemplative living," alternatively, includes that, but also much more. Morissette can sing "thank you India" because her contemplation has taken her beyond finding God's presence in her own life to finding God's presence in the world beyond her everyday experience. And Morissette thanks India not only because of her contemplation of its people and culture, but also because she discovered something extremely important in volunteering to serve the poor along with Mother Teresa's Missionaries of Charity.

Having done the same myself, I found the satisfaction of serving the poor in Mother Teresa's home for the dying. But there was also something even more special about that experience. Here we were, strangers from all over the world, working together with the sisters to wash clothes, to help people to the shower, to feed them if they could not feed themselves, and we knew ourselves to be doing so not in isolation, but as friends, as part of a team, as a community. Contemplative living, though it requires silence and time alone, is not an end in itself. It should make us more aware and more desirous of connecting with others.

Just to Be With You

• • • • | *The Importance of Friends and of Christian Community* | • • • •

What life have you if you have not life together?
There is no life that is not in community,
And no community not lived in praise of GOD
Even the anchorite who meditates alone,
For whom the days and nights repeat the praise of GOD,
Prays for the Church, the Body of Christ incarnate.
                              —T.S. Eliot[1]

One of the things that was characteristic of my young adulthood, besides having a lot of different jobs, was that I moved several times. Each time I moved, whether it was for college, a new job, or just a change of scenery, there were certain things I did. Find a place to live. Find a job, if I didn't already have one. Find a place to go to church. Once some practical matters were out of the way, I'd start putting some energy into getting to know some people. I'd make some judgments about whom I liked, and whom I didn't, and whom I might be interested in spending some of my free time with. I started looking for *friends*.

This is usually not something we think about too much. It just seems to come naturally. And, in truth, it does. It is not only the desire to be with God that is "written in the human heart," as the Catholic

Catechism says. We also have a natural desire to be with and befriend other people, sometimes as a result of sharing a common cause or belief, sometimes just because we enjoy being with them.

None of us can live complete lives without friends, and most of your Facebook "friends" probably don't count. Ask yourself: How many of them do you see or talk to on a regular basis? Indeed, years ago, when members of my particular generation, X, were asked who in their life was more important, their friends or their parents, the overwhelming majority said their friends. Though a smaller percentage of the current young adult generation might answer this way, it is still the case that when Jerry Maguire said "you complete me" he was expressing something that should not just apply to a fiancé or spouse, but that we should also be able to say about our closest friends.

Depending on our makeup, some of us will have many close friends, some only a few, but no matter what type of person you are, these friends will complement you in some way. That means more than just offering each other compliments like, "Gee your hair looks nice," or "I like your tie." It's more like a feeling that for reasons you might not even fully understand, that without that person or those persons in your life, you'd be missing something important.

Perhaps the most-remembered line in the hit comedy *As Good As It Gets*, is the one spoken by Melvin, the socially inept romance novelist, to Carol, the waitress, who may be his only friend. At dinner, Melvin tries to pay Carol a compliment, but it goes terribly wrong. Carol decides that maybe she should leave before it gets any worse. Faced with the possibility of losing her, Melvin is finally able to put it succinctly, admitting, "You make me want to be a better man." Carol is silent for a moment before confessing, "That's maybe the best compliment of my life." It's the kind of compliment that true friendships are meant to elicit. We all should have a sense that, because of our friends, we are a better people.

In chapter three I used *Buffy the Vampire Slayer* and *Good Will Hunting* as illustrations of the fact that each of us has a unique calling or vocation. Buffy and Will both have a gift that sets them apart from everybody else. But this is not the only gift they have. As much as they try to go it alone—Buffy because she wants to keep her friends from harm; Will because he doesn't want anybody to come close enough to be able to hurt him like his father did—their stories remind us that even the most extraordinary and talented people cannot do without the companionship, love, and help of their friends. When Chuckie finishes his "heart-to-heart" talk with Will, he says, "Now I don't know much, but I know that." What he's saying is that, as smart as Will is, there are some things only his friends can teach him. Only they know him well enough, only they care about him enough, to fill in the blanks of his life. Will may be able to solve complex mathematical equations, but Chuckie has a better grasp of the calculus of the heart: They need each other.

The same is true of Buffy and her band of "scoobies." No matter how dangerous the mission, and despite the fact that Buffy is the one with the superpowers, her friends rarely allow her to leave them behind. And it's not always Buffy that saves the day. Sometimes her friends end up saving her.

Buffy's need for her friends is made dramatically apparent at the end of the fourth season of the show. In the final episodes, Buffy contemplates facing Adam, her half-machine, half-human enemy, whom she knows, based on previous experience, will be difficult, if not impossible, to beat. Nevertheless, she decides she must face him, but insists that her friends stay behind. Willow, her best friend, warns that without them she's liable to have her arms ripped off. When Buffy still insists on going alone, Willow retorts, "Oh, great, and then when you have your new 'no arms' we can all say, 'Gee, it's a good thing we weren't getting in the way of that!'" The argument continues. Buffy tries to explain that she always needs them, just not this time, because it's too dangerous.

They persist, and she challenges them to tell her how they can help. When they simply fall silent, Buffy leaves, grumbling, "I guess I'm starting to understand why there's no ancient prophecy about a Chosen One and her friends."

The next day, more clear-headed, and less angry, they try to figure out a strategy for defeating Adam. Each has individual suggestions about what he or she could contribute to a solution. Giles, the former high-school librarian and Buffy's "watcher" knows of a spell that might paralyze Adam temporarily, but while he speaks the language in which it is written, he doesn't have the experience with witchcraft necessary. Willow, who is a witch (a good one), has the experience, but can't speak the language. And since all this would need to be done at close range, even if they were somehow to figure out how to do it, it would require all of them to evade the guards and accomplish all these things quickly, without any one of them being incapacitated in any way. None of them alone can succeed; their only chance is to do it together. And still, they're likely to get themselves killed.

Xander, the most "normal" of the scoobies and who has no special powers but has been Willow's most loyal friend since childhood, has been left out of this equation and desperately quips, "No problem. All we need is combo-Buffy. Her with her strength, Giles's multilingual know-how, and Willow's witchy power." They all look at him, ready to thank him for another unhelpful suggestion, until they suddenly realize that he has come up with the answer. An "enjoining" spell by which briefly Buffy would have her own powers enhanced by the brains of Giles, the magical powers of Willow, and the heart of the quick-thinking and courageous Xander would be their best chance of success. They find that the way to win is by counting on what has always sustained them up to this point, the ways in which each of their talents complement the others', allowing them to be better than they could possibly be on their own. And *together* they do succeed.

This theme is brought out even more strongly in J.R.R. Tolkien's *The Lord of the Rings*, which has become more widely known thanks to Peter Jackson's award-winning film series. One of the major themes of this epic is importance of fellowship, of friendship. While this is apparent in the many friendships throughout, even the elf Legolas and dwarf Gimli overcome the traditional animosity of their races to become the best of friends, there are few characters in the history of literature that so epitomize friendship as does Samwise Gamgee, best friend to the ring-bearer, Frodo Baggins. In many ways, not only the well-being of his friend, but the entire fate of their world, Middle-earth, rests on his shoulders—in the end, quite literally.

Frodo, after witnessing how the ring he is carrying can corrupt and endanger even his friends, tries to set off alone in a boat, in order to protect the rest of them from its dangers. Sam, however, who can't swim, stubbornly jumps into the water behind him, forcing Frodo to bring him along or watch him drown. Thus, Frodo does not set out on his mission to destroy the ring alone, and it is a good thing, because, as we discover, he would not have been able to do it without Sam. Sam saves Frodo from danger more than once on their journey, and even ends up bearing the ring himself for a time. Remarkably, Sam is little affected by it, perhaps because he represents incorruptible love and loyalty. He also ends up carrying the seriously weakened Frodo on his shoulders for the final part of their journey.

Strangely, Frodo's success also depends in the end on the fact that he insists on allowing Gollum, who is friend to neither he nor Sam, to travel with them. We feel badly for Gollum because, as a previous possessor of the ring, his very being has been corrupted by it. He is obsessed with having back what he calls "my precious," and thinks of little else. Yet, he is partially transformed for the good because of the mercy, even friendship, which Frodo shows him. It is only Frodo, burdened by carrying the ring himself, who can even come close to understanding him. Sam would just as soon kill Gollum, or cast him off, thinking he means them both only ill, but Frodo insists on letting him come along. The ironic twist is that in the end, (again, spoiler alert) when Frodo finds himself overtaken by the ring's power and unable to destroy it, it is Gollum who in his madness is unable to see someone else take full possession of the ring and bites off the finger on which Frodo has placed the ring. In doing so Gollum falls to his death in the fires of Mordor and destroys the ring in the process. Frodo's mercy, however indirectly, saves him from being corrupted. And it is only because of this, the power of Sam's friendship to get him where he could not have arrived on his own, and the efforts of their friends in other places, that the survival of Middle-earth is ensured.

• • •

In admittedly dramatic fashion, these stories tell us something about the nature of true friendship, which is something we all need, but we sometimes stop short of. Being a true friend, and allowing others to be that kind of friend to you is dangerous. It means exposing yourself to another person in a way similar to the way in which I spoke of "being naked" before God previously. Having close friends means both being loved deeply, but it also means having people in our lives who know where our vulnerabilities lie. Just as no one can love us like our closest friends, no one can hurt us like they can either. This knowledge, especially if we have been hurt, can cause us to put a limit on how much we really let someone get to know us, especially if a former friend has used what he or she knows against us.

Yet what the stories of Buffy and Frodo suggest to us is, that no matter how noble it might seem, friendship is not about protecting our friends from pain or danger. Complete strangers could do as much. Friendship is about allowing others to know us, and to make their own decisions about whether they want to brave the potential pain or danger that might come with being our friend. Shielding our friends from such harm can seem selfless, but often enough it is motivated by the more selfish fear of losing them.

What our closest friends do for us is to teach us true selflessness. We learn that while it might be safer for them if we keep them out, true friendship means letting them in. We cannot decide for them what they are willing to suffer with us and for us. While we certainly don't want to see our friends suffer, friendship isn't about protecting each other from pain so much as it is about helping each other to become what God has called us to be.

If you're a fan of the Spiderman movies, you might remember that at the end of the first movie, Peter decides that because he *is* Spiderman and must be true to that calling, he must make Mary Jane (whom he loves) think that he doesn't love her in order to protect her from the danger of being his girlfriend. But, by the end of the second movie, having figured out what's been going on, Mary Jane turns up at Peter's door. She challenges him and argues that if he respects her, he would let her make her own decision to love him or not. And if there will be risks, she argues, she'll be willing to face them with him. She says, "I love you. So here I am—standing in your doorway. I have always been standing in your doorway. Isn't it about time somebody saved your life?"[2]

Not a bad expression of what we might wish for all our closest relationships.

This is not to say, of course, that being a true friend doesn't at times involve having to let someone go, and enduring the pain and loneliness of not having them around as much as we are accustomed to. Chuckie puts on a brave face in his words to Will about his desire to show up at his house one day and not find him there, but he doesn't make Will's choice for him. If Will decides to stay with him and their other friends in Boston, Chuckie will keep coming to pick him up, day after day. But he also finds peace and even joy amid the sadness of not finding him there, because he knows it means that Will is on the way both to allowing the girlfriend he wouldn't let too close love him, and to becoming his best self by discovering what it is he's meant to do with the talents he's been given.

Indeed, sometimes we are blessed with relationships and friendships in our lives which not only give us joy and make us better, but also help to prepare us for something else. When I moved to South Carolina after returning from my year overseas, I hardly knew what to expect. Except for having once driven through the state, I had never even been there before. It was a new start for me. My relationship with Sarah ended a couple of months before my return, and I was literally all on my own. I even remember thinking that, since nobody knew me, I could be a different person. I could start going by another name, give myself a nickname, or start introducing myself by my middle name. I could start doing things that people at home would think uncharacteristic, not me. But, as should be apparent by now, it's not so easy to transform yourself, especially overnight. I decided it was just easier to be the same old "me." Although, admittedly, this was somewhat relative. My year removed from familiar surroundings had exposed me to many new experiences, and changed me quite a bit.

So, besides getting settled, I soon set about the task of making some new friends. I became close to several of the people with whom I had started the graduate program, and tried to make up for the lapse in my church-going in the past year by getting involved in the Catholic center on campus. It was there that I made several close friends, some of whom I'm still in contact with today. It was there that I met Meg, who, you might remember, made me aware of the youth ministry job I would later take, and also where I was told whom to contact about teaching religious education at a nearby parish.

I enjoyed my activities at the university's Catholic center, but I also felt God stirring that desire to give retreats to or teach high school students, as I had done in the past. I arranged a meeting with the youth ministry director in the parish. Remarkably, she already had six people who had volunteered to help that year. I was excited by the prospect of working with such a large team. She, on the other hand, as she admitted to me only some months later after we'd become close friends, had been prepared to suggest I try another parish, since they already had more help than they needed. But we hit it off almost immediately, and when I told her about my desire and my past experience, she couldn't say no. A few years later, she was one of the first people I told of my decision to apply to become a Jesuit, and the first I asked to write a recommendation for me.

The result was a dream team of sorts. We eight became fast friends and quickly discovered how well our skills complemented one another's in our work with the parish's youth. The youth program not only grew and improved, but so did we, because of our care for the young people of the parish and each other. The total impact on my life seemed disproportionate to the amount of time it lasted—only about two years. It was an experience of friendship and community I continue to cherish. I've carried the picture of the eight of us in all my moves since then, even though that experience could not be sustained. One man was in the army and was transferred, one woman got married and moved to another state, one could no longer find the time, and two of us felt called to answer the need for a youth ministry director at another parish.

Such times, such friends, are great gifts, even if, inevitably they can't be beside us forever, let alone a few years. By drawing out the best from us, they directly contribute to our becoming what God desires us to be. These were, and continue to be, some of the best and most important friends I've had in my lifetime. When I was ordained a priest in New Orleans, after celebrating Mass with friends and family my next stop was South Carolina. I needed to be with my friends there because, though I had gotten my training from the Jesuits, these were the people who had inspired and nurtured my gifts and my desires in such a way that being a Jesuit and a priest became a real option for me. There's little coincidence in my mind in the fact that four of them were with me that day, listening to the same priest talk, when God placed the question in my mind, "Why aren't you doing that?" In our work together, and in our care and love for each other, they had already, in a sense, asked me the same question.

I suppose this is in some ways why joining the Jesuits made so much sense for me. I've already told you a little bit about Saint Ignatius' conversion and pilgrim journey. It was in many ways similar to what I found in South Carolina. Both of us were young adults, making a life on our own, for the first time. Indeed, Saint Ignatius' autobiography is not just a story about becoming a saint; it is also the story of a young man becoming an adult. And, like me, Ignatius found a very special group of friends, who helped bring out the best in each other—among them, in his case, Saint Francis Xavier and Blessed Peter Faber! The idea of forming the community called the Society of Jesus was born as much out of Saint Ignatius' inspiration as it was of his friendship with them and the other "first companions." Had they not been such good friends, wishing to remain so, they might each have pursued God's will separately.

. . .

But with all this friend-making and friendship sustaining, how do we find the time for the kind of contemplative living I spoke of in the last chapter? Well, as fun as just being with our friends can be, time spent blowing off steam, laughing, and just enjoying each other's company will all start to feel empty if that is all our friendships provide. The fruits of our contemplation, the things we start to become aware of around us and within us, should be things that are shared and nurtured with our friends. True friends are not those—and we all have some people like this in our lives too—that seem to switch off whenever things get a little bit too serious. We need people who want to hear about the things that amaze us, who are willing to be there with us when we are hurting and, since we are serious about growing in our spiritual life, who will pray with us. I was fortunate to find this with my friends in South Carolina, and it's no coincidence that I found it at church.

This is why the people who claim to be spiritual but not religious may be confusing things a bit. Because what this usually means is that they believe that one can maintain a spiritual life without being part of a community. That may have worked for a few hermit monks over the centuries, but it's not going to work for most of us, unless we choose to make a radical commitment to dedicating our lives to nothing but God. Most of us have too many attachments to life in the "real world" to make so complete a break. And, even then, few of us could stand the loneliness. We need others to help us along in our spiritual journey. They provide the missing pieces we can't discover on our own. They are also some of the most concrete signs of God's presence in our lives.

When I was a child, the movement and the music of Mass bored me as much as it spoke to me of the presence of God. But the part of Mass I always loved was the Sign of Peace. This, I knew, spoke somehow of the way things should be—all of us not strangers, but a community of believers, smiling, taking each other's hands, and wishing each other peace. Though as an adult I now see how artificial all this can be, it still serves to remind us of what we are meant to be for each other as human beings, and as Christians. The writer Anne Lamott, in an essay where she tells why she makes her young son go to church, says "that I want to give him what I found in the world, which is to say a path and a little light to see by."[3] She claims she has found this path, like many of the people she knows in her community of faith, and she admits there can be all kinds of them—Buddhist, Jewish, or Christian traditions. Her particular Christian church, which she describes as "funky," is filled with people she says, "who are working for peace and freedom, who are out there on the streets and inside praying, and they are home writing letters, and they are at the shelters with giant platters of food."[4] She finds comfort in them and in fact credits them with her survival, "When I was at the end of my rope, the people at St. Andrew tied a knot in it for me and helped me hold on. The church became my home, in the old meaning of *home*—that it's where, when you show up, they have to let you in."[5]

Not all of us have a church like that, though we should. But we can't do without a community through which we participate and who will tie the knots in our ropes. You may find that you have such a community right where you live, if you just do a little searching and asking around. If you were fortunate to have once had such a community, but have now moved to a place where you are having trouble finding its equal, you may have to adjust your expectations. Or, you may find that God is calling you to help build that kind of community for others.

. . .

This is a crucial moment in the spiritual life. Much of what has been said up until now might give the impression of lots of pious navel-gazing, focused mostly on *me*, and how *I* can grow, be better and benefit. But what friendship and community teach us is that the spiritual life should eventually reach a tipping point at which it is more about what we can give than what we can get. It might take a while to reach this point, but along the way you should find your journey with God pointing you outward, as well as inward. You should find that your desire to be with God not only leads you to prayer, but also puts you into the company of those who are God for you. And despite the very human failings of our church communities, they are still the place where you are most likely to find this, even if it's not *exactly* as you'd like it to be.

Our Christian community, as important as it is to sustaining our spiritual lives, should not limit us to a building, a city, or even a state. It should open us up to those with whom we share this planet all over the world. It should provide us with a means of *solidarity*, a sense that because we are members of a human family, created by God, we are all connected and even responsible for each other. This is an important point at which contemplative living and life in a community intersect. (And chances are: You're already there!) We contemplate not only our little part of the world, but the whole world, and the ways in which it is revealed to us. In an era of widespread global travel and worldwide communication, it's not very difficult to know what's going on in other parts of the world. We may even have been fortunate enough to experience how people in other parts of the world live. But how do we maintain and nurture a sense of connection with them? This is a difficult question to answer, and those who have this sense of connection have arrived at it in many different ways. In the next chapter, I'll speak about how developing our spiritual lives, getting out and being there for others, is one way. But it also might come simply through a moment of grace on a street corner, as Thomas Merton, one of the best known contemplative monks of the twentieth century describes.

If you think monks live boring, carefree, and even unimportant lives, Thomas Merton is someone you need to get to know. His autobiography, *The Seven Storey Mountain*, is not only a classic of spiritual literature; it is a compelling story of how one young man found God in the modern world. And his decision to answer God's call to a life made up largely of silence and prayer is ultimately what made him famous. Thought at times he felt the need to live as a hermit, his contemplative life ultimately opened him more and more to the ways in which God was revealed in other people, and the events of his time (1915–1968). Though, like Gerard Manley Hopkins, he at times struggled with the demands of the religious life he had chosen, spending most of his time in his monastery in Gethsemani, Kentucky, it gave him an insight into things he might not otherwise have had.

He was one of the most popular writers of his time, writing not only on spirituality and prayer, but also social and political life in the United States, where he lived, and in the rest of the world. But, for me, one of his most profound insights comes in his description in his book *Conjectures of a Guilty Bystander* of a realization he had while standing on a street corner one day:

> In Louisville, at the corner of Fourth and Walnut, in the center of the shopping district, I was suddenly overwhelmed with the realization that I loved all those people, that they were

mine and I theirs, that we could not be alien to one another even though we were total strangers. It was like waking from a dream of separateness, of spurious self-isolation in a special world, the world of renunciation and supposed holiness. The whole illusion of a separate holy existence is a dream.[6]

This is one of the best definitions of solidarity that I know. This experience, instead of making Merton feel separate from or superior to others, instead, made him at one with them. A true spiritual life, he realized, meant his belonging to God and to others, and they to him:

It is a glorious destiny to be a member of the human race, though it is a race dedicated to many absurdities and one which makes terrible mistakes: yet, with all that, God Himself gloried in becoming a member of the human race. A member of the human race! To think that such a commonplace realization should suddenly seem like news that one holds the winning ticket in a cosmic sweepstake.

I have the immense joy of being *man*, a member of a race in which God Himself became incarnate. As if the sorrows and stupidities of the human condition could overwhelm me, now I realize what we all are. And if only everybody could realize this! But it cannot be explained. There is no way of telling people that they are all walking around shining like the sun.[7]

Merton's experience illustrates that once we get in the habit of seeing God present in our lives, something becomes especially apparent: The way in which God is most present in our lives is through other people. While God's presence revealed to us in other ways can teach us a lot about ourselves and about God, our knowledge can never be complete unless we learn to find God present in other people. It is no mistake that God chose to become incarnate in history as a human being instead of a burning bush or as an apparition of some kind. While ghosts might have been enough to save Ebenezer Scrooge, it wasn't going to be enough to save the human race. The popular song from the '90s by Joan Osborne asked the question, "What if God was one of us?" Well, from a Christian perspective, part of the answer to that question is that God *was* one of us. But the more important part of that question for us is: What if?

From the earliest days of Christian thought, it became clear that the fact that God became incarnate in the person of Jesus Christ not only changed our understanding of God, but it also changed our understanding of what it means to be human. Since God was one of us, said some of the church fathers and mothers, this meant that as human beings we have been divinized in some way. No, we have not become gods, but the likeness of God within us is now apparent in us in such a way that it cannot be ignored. And that is what the greatest contemplatives have discovered.

Thomas Merton realized that he had been given a glimpse into the truth of who we are to each other because of our relationship to God. He kind of sums up the "what if?" by saying:

> Then it was as if I suddenly saw the secret beauty of their hearts…the core of their reality, the person that each one is in God's eyes. If only they could all see themselves as they really *are*. If only we could see each other that way all the time. There would be no more war, no more hatred, no more cruelty, no more greed…[8]

Thomas Merton was right. If we all allowed ourselves to see each other in this way, our friendships would be deeper, our communities would be stronger and more vibrant, we would truly be the church of Christ, and we would do many things differently. Our world would be connected, not just by global communication networks but, more importantly, by a sense of solidarity and responsibility for each other.

CHAPTER NINE

Desire to Show Your Face

••••••••••••| *God in the Great Outdoors* | ••••••••••••

Be the change you want to see in the world.
—Mohandas Gandhi

The more deeply we become involved in the life of God and the lives of others, the more we realize that, as beautiful as the things we contemplate might be, and as much as we might enjoy just hanging out with our friends, we are also expected to take an active role in our world. Indeed, if you've ever watched one of those movies about the life of Jesus like *Jesus of Nazareth*, besides noticing the somewhat creepy fact that Jesus never blinks, you probably also noticed that Jesus is almost always outdoors. Sure, he takes time to pray, to rest, and to visit with friends, but mostly he's out in the open where he can see people, and people can see him. This is a model of the way life is supposed to be.

But it's not just a matter of getting outdoors. After all, you could spend most of your time outside, and still not accomplish much of anything. No, having become conscious that our lives are lived in response to our desire for God, and God's desire for us, we must, like Thomas Merton, open ourselves to the working of God's grace. God's grace is nurtured in prayer and helps us to be more aware of the gifts God has given us. Then, it moves us beyond ourselves, beyond that which is familiar and comfortable, into a world of challenges and surprises where God uses us for his glory, and the good of others.

It should be obvious to you by now that I'm the kind of person who spent a lot of my life looking to be entertained. I grew up watching a lot of TV. I've seen more movies than most people. I discovered early on, when the most popular games were Space Invaders and Pac-Man, that I had to be really careful about video games—I could get lost in them for hours. And that was all before the Internet which, for me, has been a blessing and a curse. None of these are necessarily problematic in and of themselves, but it is important that we become aware that we live in a time when passive entertainment has become more and more a part of our world, and that each of us has to reflect on how much time we devote to it, and the extent to which it interferes with our work, our relationships and our response to God's grace.

If you've read the Harry Potter series, or seen the movies (I've done both), you might remember the Mirror of Erised, which appeared in *Harry Potter and the Sorcerer's Stone*. Harry discovers the mirror, in which he sees the image of himself happily standing with the parents he never knew, killed when he was just an infant. This image is so consoling, that he finds himself going back over and over again to spend time just sitting in front of the mirror. What harm could there be in that?

The mirror, however, is not meant to be enjoyed. What we learn is that actually it is to be used as a trap, as a means of protecting the Sorcerer's Stone. On it, is the inscription, "erised stra ehru oyt ube cafru oyt on wohsi" which, when read backwards says, *"I show not your face, but your heart's desire."* The image one sees in the mirror is one's deepest desire. Thus, the one whose desire was to become powerful using the Sorcerer's Stone would see him or herself doing just that, and would be ever searching for clues in it as to how to make that come about, rather than actually accomplishing it. Otherwise, as consoling as it is for Harry, and for Ron, who sees himself as head boy winning the Quidditch Cup, it is a dangerous indulgence. Dumbledore explains: "Men have wasted away before it, entranced by what they have seen, or been driven mad, not knowing if what it shows is real or even possible."[1]

Many of our passive entertainments, the Internet especially, are filled with potential "Mirrors of Erised." Our desires can run amok in all the pleasures and distractions that the Internet provides and promises. The possibility of becoming lost, living in a virtual world instead of a real one, is very real. And one can find lots of ways to justify it. Even as I write this book, I find myself taking frequent breaks to check my e-mail, or see what's going on with my Facebook friends. It used to be that one could escape these things merely by leaving the home or office. But now, even that is no guarantee. I'm sure you've noticed how many people these days are caught up in the world of their handheld devices, even when they are outdoors! You might even have noticed that habit in yourself. These days, we can carry our "Mirror of Erised" with us everywhere we go! And, as Dumbledore warns, that's not necessarily a good thing.

I know this might seem like the equivalent of telling you that rock music is evil, which I don't believe by the way, but bear with me for a minute. If the spiritual life manifests itself in the kind of contemplative living that I spoke about in chapter seven, and if it is meant to nurture true friendships and build the kinds of community I spoke of in chapter eight, does spending all one's free time outdoors checking e-mail, surfing the Web, or watching the latest episode of *The Daily Show* help the spiritual life, or hinder it?

I love technological gadgets. I know I could easily become one of those people who even when out in the world, is only contemplating the computer display in front of him, and missing out on the beauty of God's creation and the beauty of others. So, while I'd be lying if I told you that I wasn't tempted to buy the latest iPhone or BlackBerry, I have so far resisted because I'm already aware of how much time I can spend with what's available to me indoors. I haven't spoken too much about spiritual discipline in this book, but one of the most basic "rules" is to be aware of the things that can most distract us from God, and to set limits for ourselves with regard to our use of them. It is out of that awareness, and not out of some belief in the evils of technology, that I speak.

Several years ago, I got myself enmeshed in the world of blogs and blogging. It seemed like an exciting opportunity to reach out to people, to do ministry, in a whole new way. It was also an opportunity to put my writing skills to work. My blog dealt mostly with things Christian and Catholic, and my audience was predominantly people who were interested in those things. It opened up dialogues with people about the church, faith, and life lived with God and in God's service. I became part of a whole new community of Catholic friends, fellow bloggers who were passionate about the same kinds of things I was. People would write me and ask me questions. I came to understand it as one of my ministries. At the height of my blogging activity, my blog was even voted, "Best Blog by a Seminarian." How could that be a problem?

Well, in order to get there, I had gotten to the point at which I was updating my blog just about every day. I was also reading, and commenting on, about twenty or thirty other blogs on a regular basis. And this wasn't the only thing that kept me indoors. I spent a good eight to ten hours per week sitting in my seminary classes, and about as much time sitting doing my homework. There were also other writing projects to which I had to give some time. If I could convince myself of the importance of my Internet ministry, that meant I could spend much of my time indoors, not getting out doing much of anything else. I realized that this was a grave and dangerous temptation, especially for me. I might spend several days keeping myself busy with these various things, and then realize that except for class and a few mandatory things, I had not left the house! If you'll recall those Jesus movies again, you'll remember that the Apostles imitated Jesus in spending most of their time outdoors as well. Spending all day at home, I realized, was not what a disciple of Jesus—which is what we are all called to be— would be doing!

It wasn't just the matter of being indoors so much, either. I also slowly began to realize how this one way of connecting with people electronically—and this is why I've found I've also had to limit my use of social networking sites like Facebook—could really start to jeopardize my availability to the people around me—the people with whom I lived, the people to whom I was ministering, and my friends. This became especially apparent when one friend apologized to me for being out of touch. He said that since he had been reading my blog, it didn't seem like we had been out of touch for so long!

The Internet provides helpful tools for staying connected with people, but we have to be careful they don't just give us the *illusion* of being a part of people's lives, of having acted, when we really haven't. As I suggested in the last chapter, while our social networking "friends" might be people we want to keep track of, the majority are not and cannot be the kind of friends we need. You'll remember that I said early on in the book that a true spiritual life not only connects us with God, but also inspires us to get involved in the lives of others. We have an obligation to be there for those around us.

This isn't always easy. For the last four years I lived in a part of Boston where, when I went out to meet up with friends or run errands or even go to church, I couldn't do it without passing several homeless people begging for money. Sometimes I gave one or two of them some change, sometimes I tried to avoid them, but always I was troubled by the overwhelming need they represented. As much as I wanted to help them all, I knew it was impossible. In this same part of Boston, there were (and are) also always people trying to recruit others to their cause—*do you have a couple of minutes to help protect the environment, human rights, or to help needy children?* I know they meant well, but nevertheless I couldn't help but find them obnoxious, and many times I ignored them.

There are so many worthy causes and endeavors to which we could give our time and talents, so many needs in our own communities, never mind in the world, that we can feel overwhelmed. Indeed, the great temptation might be to stay indoors rather than expose ourselves to the sea of need which lies just outside. Given that there is so much, how can we know exactly what to do?

As a Jesuit and a priest, I struggle with this as much as anybody else. Just looking around at the men in my community, and all the things that they are doing, I know that there are lots of worthwhile things to which I could give my time. And this is not to mention the many unanticipated needs I might encounter just getting out of the house and being with people. Sometimes the temptation to stay home, using the computer or watching a movie is not because of laziness, but it's because I already have plenty to do. An unexpected encounter might steal away the time I had set aside to, for example, prepare my homily for Mass on Sunday, or to get a retreat talk ready. I hate the feeling of being torn between thinking that I really need to be there for someone, and wanting to get away because I have something else I was planning on doing at that time. I find this happening even more often since I've been ordained a priest. So, rather than cause someone to feel that I don't care about them, I find myself asking God to pick up the slack for me. If I'm not as prepared for my homily Sunday morning as I would like, I'm saying to God beforehand, "This is your fault, so you'd better help me out."

But this still doesn't get at the core issue. Shouldn't my growth in the spiritual life have started to give me an idea of what I'm supposed to do and what I'm not? Well, again, here's where community is a help. As a Jesuit, though admittedly I don't always look at it this way, I'm lucky. Each day, when I walk out my bedroom door, I immediately encounter a group of people to whom I owe certain things. I should not just leave things lying around the house, I should put them away. If the dishwasher is full, I should run it. If it's finished, I should empty it. If I see someone else emptying it, I should help. If someone has just returned from buying groceries for the house, I should help them carry them in. If someone's not feeling well, I should ask how they are doing, and ask if I can get something for them.

In my early days as a Jesuit, I didn't always do so well with such things. *I have a paper to finish writing*, I might think, *I don't have time to empty the dishwasher!* Or worse: *I'm always doing that; let somebody else do it for a change!* Fortunately, the example of a few guys in the house, who were *always* generous about such things, convinced me to try to do the same. A couple minutes away from paper-writing, I realized, wasn't going to make the difference a few minutes spent doing something for the people I live with could. And so I developed certain habits and instincts for acting generously which affected my life not only inside the house, but outside.

These may seem like little things which have nothing to do with the spiritual life, but these are spiritual practices, especially when we do them not merely out of a sense of duty, or because it's our job (in Jesuit houses, we all have certain assigned jobs), but simply because we love and care about others, and God. Saint Thérèse of Lisieux built her whole spirituality around such practices. What she called the "little way" consisted precisely in the small, ordinary things we do for each other every day. As a young woman living in a monastery, this *was* her spiritual life. Pope John Paul II even recognized her profound spiritual wisdom by pronouncing her a doctor of the church, a title given to only a handful of theologians and spiritual writers in the church's two thousand years. And you can be sure that Thomas Merton's moment of grace at the corner of Fourth and Walnut didn't just change the way he looked at the world, it changed the way he acted as well. How could we not change the way we act toward one another after an epiphany like that?

So, the trick is to start small. If we're spending every day trying to save the world, it probably won't be long until we're retreating again to the comfort of our televisions and computer screens. So, it might be helpful to have a look at the apostles again. What are they doing while they are outside? A good rule of thumb for reading the Gospel is to presume that what Jesus is telling the apostles they should do is what we should do.

Of course, we also have to adapt it to our own situations. Few of us will be spending our days casting out demons and unclean spirits, but we may, eventually, after having matured in the spiritual life, help others with spiritual direction or, at least, engage in spiritual conversations with people that might help them discern God's voice a little more clearly. Yet, before we get there, it will probably be easier to try something even more simple and practical than that, engaging, for example, in what the Christian tradition has called the corporal works of mercy. These are the most basic Christian acts, the things that Jesus told the apostles to do for others which, in doing so, he said, they would also be doing for him: Feed the hungry, give drink to the thirsty, clothe the naked, shelter the homeless, visit the sick, visit those in prison, and bury the dead. Jesus also insisted that the apostles be agents of healing and reconciliation. One of the signs that we have advanced in the spiritual life, then, is that we will have incorporated the regular exercise of some of these works into our daily life.

All of them might not be for us. Those who have experienced trauma as the result of having a family member in prison, for example, might find prison visits too hard to take. But we should find ourselves involved in the lives of those in need. And notice that these are called "corporal" works. This means there is an expectation that we be there, bodily. We can make donations of clothes or money to help make these things happen, but as we have found others to be the God-with-us that we needed, the corporal works give us an opportunity to be God present to someone else.

This is what we find when we look not only at what Jesus told the apostles to do, but also at what God does and is for us in Jesus. God could operate the universe like Bruce in *Bruce Almighty*, who answers prayers by sitting at a keyboard and clicking a mouse. Like the IT person for a divine Internet, God could just sit at his computer all day, running things from there. This would be a lot more efficient than the messy work of getting involved in the complexities of human affairs. Yet, when things got out of whack, he decided that the best way of dealing with the problem was by taking part in the human race, as one of us himself. Suddenly, God had a human face, one which he wanted to show to everyone. *God's desire was and is to show his face.* So that we may know him, find him, and let us be found in return.

God showed his face. God came among us as a human being, and gave us an example to follow. So, between what Jesus did, and what he told the apostles to do, we can come up with a pretty good plan of action for the spiritual life.

Though it might seem obvious and easy, we have already seen that there are many things in our lives that can get in the way of our fulfilling the first requirement. We have to *show up*. In other words, we have to be ready and willing to do something, not put God off until we finish our next game of *Halo* or answer our e-mails. We also have to be willing to depend upon God for what we need. Jesus didn't come to earth fully grown, but as a vulnerable child who, as the Gospel tells us, people in power were out to kill, rather than to see him grow up. Think John Connor in the *Terminator* movies and TV show, and you get the idea (except that Jesus' mother Mary wasn't wielding automatic weapons). So, like John Connor, Jesus needed to have people looking out for him, because there was a lot he just wouldn't be able to do himself.

This dependence upon God wasn't just a result of Jesus' days as an infant. It was the way he operated his entire life. He knew that God would provide—often through the generosity of others—and he wanted others to believe the same. So, his instructions to the apostles in the Gospel of Mark don't come as a complete surprise: "He called the twelve and began to send them out two by two, and gave them authority over unclean spirits. He ordered them to take nothing for their journey except a staff; no bread, no bag, no money in their belts; but to wear sandals and not to put on two tunics" (Mark 6:7–9). These days, we might not be able to manage such radical dependence on God and others' generosity, but we can at least bring some of that spirit to making ourselves available for what God might want us to do.

So, in addition to showing our faces, and developing the habits of generosity I already spoke of, how can we depend upon others' generosity, if we don't practice it ourselves? We should start listening for God's voice. Now, don't panic. As I've said before, unless you are luckier than most—and not crazy—you are not listening for an actual, audible voice here. This is more likely to take the form of listening to your desires. There's a little trust, and a sort of recklessness, involved here. You have to trust that all the things you have been doing up until now as far as deepening your relationship with God, have had some effect. They have put you more in tune with the ways in which God has been and is at work in your life. So, when you find yourself asking the question: What is it that God wants me to do? You also should be aware of your desire to do certain types of things. Saint Ignatius, you might remember, wanted to be like Saint Francis and Saint Dominic. So, when he set out on his journey, he did the sorts of things that he thought they would do, but because he was Ignatius, he did those things in a unique way. So, while some of the things he did were the "same old thing" that other saints had done before him, other things, such as his penchant for spiritual conversation, and the spiritual exercises he developed for himself and others, carried his unique stamp. He wasn't even the first person to write something called *The Spiritual Exercises,* but the way he fashioned them was according to the experience of young adult conversion he was having at the time.

Similarly, you'll find that many of the holy desires that you have aren't necessarily unique. We should all, for example, desire what is sometimes referred to as the "Godspell grace." It's called that because it is a desire expressed in "Day by Day," a song from the musical, *Godspell.* The song talks about—of course—living day by day, but also about loving God and seeing more clearly. These basic Christian desires are what motivated the saints to do many of the same types of things. But they also did their own thing or, better put, those unique things which God had chosen them to do. This is revealed in the personal desires which rise out of your spiritual life. They often take the form of an inspiration to do something only you can do, or to act on a creative idea you have. Not all such inspiration and ideas will be what God desires for you personally. So these must be measured in light of those more basic Christian desires. If the idea is to do something which you can see could very well distance you from God, there's a good chance that this is not the desire God means for you to act upon. Even if that danger doesn't seem so apparent, it may be hard to anticipate how a given course of action will affect your relationship with God. Perfect clarity is often hard to arrive at. There's always a little bit of recklessness involved in responding to God's grace, but it is better than being paralyzed by doubt or fear. Again, you have to trust that the efforts you have been making in your relationship with God will bear fruit.

The process is a little bit like the plot of one of my favorite movies, *Field of Dreams*. The main character, Ray Kinsella, is a baseball fan whose father spent some time as a minor league player. Ray lives on a farm in Iowa with his wife and daughter. One day, while walking in his cornfield, he hears a voice. He thinks somebody is trying to play a joke on him. But there's no one there. Just a voice, saying, "If you build it, he will come." At first, he thinks he's imagining things, and ignores it. Then, another day, he hears the same voice again, "If you build it, he will come." He starts to think this is something he's meant to take seriously. Build what? Who will come?

After talking with his wife, Annie, and paying attention to what things around him might be saying, he believes he's come up with an answer. Ray grew up on stories of Shoeless Joe Jackson, one of the Chicago "Black Sox," accused of throwing the 1919 World Series. Ray, who narrates parts of the film, explains that of the eight players found guilty, Jackson's actual participation seems the most in doubt, based both on testimony of the other conspirators, and the fact that he didn't seem to play any differently in the series than he normally did. Nevertheless, Jackson was banned for life from playing baseball, as the others were. Imagining a baseball field on his property, Ray decides that is what he's meant to build. As far as who will come, he believes that the field is to be a place where Shoeless Joe can somehow play baseball again. Annie helps to convince him that he's not crazy, and encourages him to do it. So, Ray plows down a portion of his cornfield and builds the equivalent of a major league baseball field, lights and all. Maybe not crazy, but definitely reckless, as the mortgagors of his property are quick to point out.

A year passes and nothing happens. The creditors are closing in, and Ray's faith is tested. Finally, one night, a baseball player shows up on the field, dressed in an old Chicago White Sox uniform. Ray goes out to meet the player who is, indeed, Shoeless Joe Jackson. Jackson expresses his gratitude for the field, and asks if he can bring some others to play along with him. Soon, many long-dead players join him, among them some others who were banned. Though there's never really any expla-nation as to how this could happen, Ray has managed to restore to these men one of the things they most loved in life. All because he took that voice seriously. Unfortunately, most people can't see the players like he, Annie, and his daughter, Karin, can. So most, including his brother-in-law, partner to the mortgage holders, think he's simply plowed his corn to build a field that goes unused.

And the voice isn't done with Ray. It tells him to "ease his pain." A shared dream with his wife leads Ray on a cross-country trip to Boston to find Terry, a once popular, but now embittered writer. He convinces Terry to return home with him, finding his family on the brink of bankruptcy.

Yet Karin, and then Terry, channeling the magic in the air, reassure Ray that things will be OK. "People will come," they say. They will come from all over, not even knowing exactly why, to see the field, and pay for the privilege. We learn that there was a reason Terry was brought there, to see what Ray can't see, including being invited beyond the outfield, to see where the magic comes from. Ray objects, arguing that it was his response to the voice—his recklessness—that got them this far. He should be allowed to go.

Shoeless Joe challenges Ray, "Is that why you did this? For you? I think you'd better stay here." Ray's recklessness can't extend to abandoning his family altogether.

As Shoeless Joe is walking off the field, he gets Ray's attention, pointing to the one player remaining on the field, the catcher. "If you build it, he will come," he reminds Ray.

"It was you," Ray says to Shoeless Joe.

"No, Ray, it was you," Shoeless Joe replies.

Earlier in the movie, Ray had explained his regret that as a boy, he had grown so tired of his father's baseball stories, that by the time he was fourteen, he refused to play catch with his dad. His father had died before he'd had a chance to make up for it. Ray realizes that though he didn't remember him looking that young, the catcher is his father, John Kinsella. John introduces himself, and thanks Ray, Annie, and Karin for letting him and the others use the field.

"Is this heaven?" John asks.

"It's Iowa," Ray replies.

"Iowa?" John answers. "I could have sworn it was heaven."

As John moves to go, Ray says, "Hey, Dad, you want to have a catch?" Annie turns on the lights, and Ray has a catch with his father. And, as the movie finishes, we see the line of headlights of the people who are also coming after all.[2]

Many of you have probably seen the movie and, if you have, it might provoke a lot of feelings in you, like it does for me. I can't even write about it without getting a little teary-eyed. This is because though it is a fantasy, so much about it touches on real human experiences that we can relate to. Like Terry's speech in *On the Waterfront*, the images and the words linger in our collective consciousness, even now, twenty years since the movie was first released. But, for me, it's also more than that.

For me, the movie is a great representation of the kind of things that happen when we act recklessly in response to God's grace.

In this case, the "if you build it, he will come" is a literal voice that leads Ray to do something completely absurd which, nevertheless, he is certain is the right thing to do. Like Peter stepping out of the boat, the only immediate logical consequence is to find himself drowning. And his faith is tested, for while a storm of debt threatens, the field appears to be just that, a field. He has to trust that God, or perhaps in this case "the voice," is eventually going to make something happen. This is not so unlike when God first calls Abraham in the Old Testament. God tells him to uproot himself, and take his whole family to a strange place, where he will make of him a great nation. Abraham's son and great nation were even longer in coming than Shoeless Joe Jackson was to Ray's Iowa cornfield.

Now, if this was all there was to it, once Shoeless Joe showed up, and brought some other players with him, the field could have also become the equivalent of a Mirror of Erised, where Ray and his family basked in the glory of long-dead baseball players, while their lives crumbled around them. Certainly, that's what others in the town thought they were doing. But Ray doesn't fall into that trap. With the help of a dream and of the voice, he sees there is more to do. At one point in the movie, he must leave the pleasures of his magical baseball field so that he can go even as far as Boston to ease someone else's pain. This is a good approximation of what Christian charity often demands of us (and Christian charity has little to do with donating money, and a lot more to do with *love*). We are challenged to put aside selfish pleasures and even sometimes to sacrifice them altogether, in order to show ourselves as God present to someone else in pain. Sometimes this will mean venturing further from home than expected!

Notice what happens as a result of Ray's willingness to listen to the voice and act on it. Shoeless Joe and his teammates get a shot at redemption. All that before it even occurs to Ray to even ask, "What's in it for me?" And that's where things become very interesting. In a sense, one could say that Ray really got it wrong from the very beginning. The "he" which the first voice spoke of wasn't Shoeless Joe, but his father. But how could we say he got it wrong, when so much good came of the things which Ray did? That's the mystery of grace. It's not an exact science. It's not always one thing or the other. What's most important is that we choose to act upon what we believe God is saying to us. God will make sure that we won't go too far off track, and a lot of good will get done in the process.

Also, don't overlook the fact that "the voice" wasn't something wholly external to Ray. It was something that rose out of his passions and desires—his passion for baseball, his trust and, most of all, his desire to be with his father.

CONCLUSION

The Greatest Thing You'll Ever Learn
• • • • • • • • • • • • • • • | *To Be With Jesus* | • • • • • • • • • • • • • • • •

I can remember sitting in a boat, feeling its rhythm as it rocked back and forth, smelling the saltiness of the sea, feeling the strength of the wood where I sat, a soft wind touching my face, and Jesus laying there at my feet, sleeping. I just sat there and watched, contemplating the man I saw before me. An ordinary man, doing one of the most ordinary things. There was nothing in how he slept to betray who he was. He could be any one of us. There was only the calm of the soundest sleep. The calm that would only become strange when the storm started to rage. But, for now, there was no storm, only an extraordinary peace. And though I knew it impossible, I thought perhaps I could stay there forever, just watching, just knowing the presence of the one I loved and the one who loved me. I could remain a bit longer, and I did. Nothing was ever said. Yet, as I returned to the concreteness of the chapel in which I prayed, I knew this prayer had changed me.

Such prayers have been rare moments for me. I'm not really sure that they are meant to come along so often, lest we not appreciate them when they do. But experiences like this remain, as strong as the most vivid memory. I recall that prayer, and I remember it as if I were really there. An encounter like this with the one who loves us stays with us, like those songs or movie moments that get stuck in our collective consciousness, reminding us who we are, and what we can be. They sustain us. In our most difficult times, the quiet necessary to make room for this kind of prayer may be impossible to come by, that's why we not only need to appreciate them when they come, but we also must store them up, so we can call upon the memories when we need them, the reminder that God is with us, and we with God, as we once realized so clearly.

Now it might still seem strange to you that sitting in a boat with a sleeping Jesus might be so consoling, but I hope that it seems less so than when you first picked up this book. This may not be the kind of experience that you can appreciate in the way that I did. You will need to (and I hope you have) use your imagination to encounter Jesus in a way that speaks to you, and your desires. When my fellow novices and I were taught this kind of imaginative prayer in our first year as Jesuits, we weren't told exactly what kind of experiences to have. Indeed, my spiritual director seemed to think some of my experiences a bit strange. But we were told something that was very helpful. We were encouraged to put aside the unblinking, robe-wearing Jesus who only speaks King James English, and to imagine Jesus more as we would a friend, perhaps dressed in comfortable jeans and a T-shirt, and speaking with a Boston accent. Try it. It erases some of the distance we might feel from Jesus and, even with a Boston accent, Jesus can say what he needs to say to us.

When I first started thinking about becoming a Jesuit, I mostly prayed just to God the Father, as I think many people do. But I thought, if I'm going to become a member of the Society of *Jesus*, it might be good for me to start praying directly to Jesus more often. As a reminder, I taped the *Anima Christi*—one of Saint Ignatius' favorite prayers—on the inside cover of my prayer book:

> Soul of Christ, sanctify me.
> Body of Christ, save me.
> Blood of Christ, inebriate me.
> Water from the side of Christ, wash me.
> Passion of Christ, strengthen me.

O Good Jesus, hear me.
Within Thy wounds hide me.
Suffer me not to be separated from thee.
From the malignant enemy defend me.
In the hour of my death call me.
And bid me come unto Thee,
That with all Thy saints,
I may praise thee
Forever and ever.
Amen.[1]

I loved the way this prayer expressed the desire for all that was Jesus to be with me, and part of me. It seemed like the right kind of prayer for someone who wanted to draw closer to Jesus. I think that's why Saint Ignatius prayed it so often, and shared it with others.

There is something about praying with Jesus, and to Jesus, that we can't get when we pray to the more abstract "God," even if we pray to God the Father. We can pray to the Holy Spirit, too, but for me the dynamism of the Holy Spirit is more apparent in how God is working in the events of my daily life, and less in thinking of the Holy Spirit as someone to pray to. Only Jesus, in all his bodily humanness, speaks to me so strongly about how God is with me, and only to Jesus can I pray with the comfort of an everyday conversation, even if nothing much is said. Like in the prayer, which speaks of Jesus' body and blood, water and wounds, soul and passion, I know Jesus to be so intimately with me and part of me because I am those things too. And though what I know of God has come from my experience of worship, religious education, and prayer, among other things, the way in which I encounter God is most often in other people, people like Jesus.

Does this mean we should forget about God the Father and the Holy Spirit? Certainly not. I only emphasize this because I think a lot of people are like I was, before I made the conscious decision to pray to Jesus more, praying to a more generalized, and less intimate God. I think this is why, up until that time, while I was pretty confident in God's love for me, I hadn't quite figured out what it meant for me to love God. After all, the all-powerful God didn't really need me to love him, right? This was interesting too, because it was more the opposite in my relationships with other people. I found it easy to love them, but I wasn't always so sure that I could be confident in their love for me. Indeed, I would often presume the worst. When meeting someone I really liked, I would take for granted that they did not feel the same way about me.

Praying to Jesus made a significant difference in these things. As my prayer experience of being in the boat with Jesus suggests, Jesus helped me to know what it meant to love God, through loving him, but also by seeing in the Gospel and by the use of imagination in prayer, his love for God the Father. I asked him to help free me from that doubt about whether others could love me, or even like me, as I did them. I sought this gift many times, and yet I kept finding my anxiety there, tugging at my confidence about my relationships with others. I eventually decided that like Saint Paul who, having received no satisfaction from God despite numerous requests that God remove the "thorn in his side" (he never says what it was), I would just have to learn to live with it. So, I stopped praying about it for a while, and did my best to try and let myself be loved in spite of it. Then, one day, I simply noticed it was gone. That's not to say that I've been freed from my many other insecurities, but I've found it a lot easier to let others love me since then.

My suspicion is that if you were to ask most people what they had the hardest time with, and they all answered honestly, the majority of people in contemporary American society would say "being loved." Even the narcissistic person—*especially* the narcissistic person—who seems to thrive on the love of others, and will tell you how much he or she is loved, needs constant reassurance of that love. For most of the rest of us, it has something to do with our drive to be independent and self-sustaining and to at least appear as if we can make it without anyone else's help. What we don't realize is that this, as much as anything else, gets in the way of that desire for love in our lives that I spoke about at the beginning of the book. We are a love-obsessed people with a love handicap.

We have to recognize our vulnerability. However, this very word illustrates the problem. We tend only to speak of our vulnerability to bad things. These days, for example, we hear a lot about our vulnerability to attack. But how often do hear people speak about our vulnerability to love? It even sounds wrong, but it shouldn't. Vulnerability to love should actually be seen as our greatest gift.

· · ·

This book in large part is about opening you up to the vulnerability of being loved, by God, and by other people. This is the most important connection we can make, whether we are contemplating our present, past, or future. This is what we truly desire, which we discover when we are able to remove at least some of those many things that get in the way, and especially when we trust God to do some of that for us. We all want to be loved, and to love, as freely as we can.

This is why Jesus is so important for us. Jesus is the person who epitomized the vulnerability necessary to love and be loved with complete freedom. He was confident in the mission that God had given him, and fulfilled it in a way that showed the consistency of his love both for God, and for the people he encountered. And he didn't hide the fact that the vulnerability to love also meant the vulnerability to persecution and pain. Yet, unlike us, especially those of us who have experienced great pain at the hands of others, he gave primacy to the vulnerability to love, recklessly risking the consequences.

Most of us know how it turned out. Jesus was betrayed by one of his friends, and abandoned by most of the rest of them. He was mistreated and mocked, found guilty of trumped-up charges, and executed on a cross. But not before his love and mercy, reconciliation, and healing, had already changed the world. Like Ray in *Field of Dreams*, he forgets to ask, "What's in it for me?" because he was compelled by his love for his father and, at least in Jesus' case, for all of us.

After I've said all that, you may not be surprised to learn that this book was inspired by two conversations with Jesus. The first took place on a grassy hill somewhere in the Holy Land of my imagination. Jesus was wearing those comfortable jeans and T-shirt I spoke of before. I was nearing the end of the eight-day silent retreat in my second year of novitiate. It was the last retreat we would make before deciding whether or not to request taking vows as a Jesuit, promising perpetual poverty, chastity, and obedience. Basically, the decision was whether or not to write a letter that expressed my desire to become a Jesuit, and remain one forever. This is what Jesus and I were talking about, more or less. I only remember one part of the conversation, because it was the most important. I asked Jesus simply, "What do you want me to do?" His answer was equally simple, "I want you to be with me." I wrote the letter, took vows, and here I am, ten years later, finishing the book which, in a lot of ways, is the story of being with Jesus, the Jesus who was always there.

The other conversation is yours. This book, as should become clear to you in a minute, is patterned on the first conversation with Jesus that Saint Ignatius encourages us to have in *The Spiritual Exercises*. He invites us to imagine speaking to Jesus as he is hanging on the cross. It might seem a strange way to have a conversation at first, but it certainly highlights Jesus' vulnerability, and it is also Ignatius' way of emphasizing one of the things he most hoped that people would walk away from *The Exercises* with: a profound sense of gratitude for all that Jesus has done and does for us.

Ignatius suggests initiating the conversation with some interesting questions like: "Why did you—God—become a human being?" and "Why should you have to die, and die for us?" But the part that I have always found most interesting, and most helpful, is what comes next. He advises the person praying to step back from the conversation for a minute and reflect on himself or herself, by asking the following three questions:

What have I done for Christ?

What am I doing for Christ?

What ought I to do for Christ?

I have spent a lot of time these past ten years reflecting on these very questions. In a way, you have also, for however long you've been reading this book. But the conversation is not finished. Ignatius has one more instruction which I can't help but find a little bit comical, but also rather appropriate. He says to turn back to Jesus and say to him "whatever comes to mind."

So, get to it! Stop moving around so much, and let him find you. He's already there. Just start talking.

NOTES

FOREWORD

1. Quoted in *A Jesuit off-Broadway: Center Stage With Jesus, Judas, and Life's Big Questions,* James Martin, S.J. (Chicago: Loyola, 2007), p. 67.

PREFACE

1. Donald Miller, *Searching For God Knows What* (Nashville: Thomas Nelson, 2004), p. 14.

INTRODUCTION

1. Death Cab for Cutie, "I Will Possess Your Heart," *I Will Possess Your Heart* (Atlantic Records, 2008).
2. U2, "I Still Haven't Found What I am Looking For," *The Joshua Tree* (Island Records, 1987).
3. *The Catechism of the Catholic Church,* 27.
4. Saint Augustine, *Confessions,* Henry Chadwick, trans. (New York: Oxford University Press, 1998), p. 3.

CHAPTER ONE

1. Budd Schulberg, *On the Waterfront* script, available on http://www.dailyscript.com/scripts/onthewaterfront.html.

CHAPTER TWO

1. Flannery O'Connor, *The Habit of Being.* Sally Fitzgerald, ed. and intro. (New York: Farrar, Straus, Giroux, 1979), p. 427.
2. Louis J. Puhl, S.J. *The Spiritual Exercises of St. Ignatius: Based On Studies in the Language of The Autograph* (Chicago: Loyola, Ignatius, 1951), p. xx.
3. *Saint Ignatius Loyola: Personal Writings.* Joseph Munitz and Philip Endean, eds. and trans. (New York: Penguin, 1996), p. 209.
4. Tracy Chapman, "Change," *Where You Live* (Atlantic Records, 2005).

CHAPTER THREE

1. Henri Nouwen, *Seeds of Hope: A Henri Nouwen Reader,* Robert Durback, ed. (New York: Image, 1997), pp. 148–149.
2. From the opening credits of *Buffy the Vampire Slayer.*
3. Matt Damon and Ben Affleck, *Good Will Hunting: A Screenplay* (New York: Hyperion, 1997), p. 134.

4. Damon and Affleck, p. 134.

5. Damon and Affleck, p. 134.

6. Søren Kierkegaard, *The Sickness Unto Death: A Christian Psychological Exposition for Upbuilding and Awakening*, Howard V. Hong and Edna H. Hong, eds., trans. (Princeton, N.J.: Princeton University Press, 1980), p. 85.

CHAPTER FOUR

1. Karl Rahner as quoted in Ronald Rolheiser, *The Holy Longing: The Search for a Christian Spirituality* (New York: Doubleday, 1999), p. 204.

CHAPTER FIVE

1. Scenes described from the movie *50 First Dates*. A transcript is available at www.script-o-rama.com/movie_scripts/f/50-first-dates-script-transcript.html.

CHAPTER SIX

1. Renée M. LaReau, *Getting a Life: How to Find Your True Vocation* (Maryknoll, N.Y.: Orbis, 2003), p. 144.

2. Joan Didion, *The Year of Magical Thinking* (New York: Knopf, 2006), p. 15.

3. Loyola, p. 289.

CHAPTER SEVEN

1. Thomas H. Johnson, ed. *The Poems of Emily Dickinson* (Cambridge, Mass.: Belknap, 1955), p. 75.

2. W.H. Gardner and N.H. MacKenzie, eds. *The Poems of Gerard Manley Hopkins* (London: Oxford, 1967), p. 90.

CHAPTER EIGHT

1. T.S. Eliot *Collected Poems 1909–1962* (New York: Harcourt, Brace Jovanovich, 1963), p. 154.

2. Scenes described from the movie *Spiderman 2*. A transcript is available at www.script-o-rama.com/movie_scripts/s/spiderman-2-script-transcript.html.

3. Anne Lamott, *Traveling Mercies: Some Thoughts on Faith* (New York: Anchor, 1999), p. 100.

4. Lamott, p. 100.

5. Lamott, p. 100.

6. Thomas Merton, *Conjectures of a Guilty Bystander* (Garden City, N.Y.: Doubleday, 1966), p. 156.

7. Merton, p. 157.
8. Merton, p. 158.

CHAPTER NINE

1. J.K. Rowling, *Harry Potter and the Sorcerer's Stone* (New York: Scholastic, 1999), p. 157.
2. Scenes described from the movie *Field of Dreams*. A transcript is available at www.script-o-rama.com/movie_scripts/f/field-of-dreams-script-transcript.html.

CONCLUSION

1. The Anima Christi can be found at http://www.ourcatholicprayers.com/anima-christi.html.

About the Author

MARK MOSSA, S.J., has served as a minister for young adults in various parts of the northeast and southern United States. He currently teaches theology at Fordham University in New York, and occasionally updates his blogs, GODsTALKed~: Pursuits of a Hyphenated Priest (http://frmarkmossasj.blogspot.com) and Spoiler Alert: God's Already There (http://lettinggodfindyou.blogspot.com) which has a soundtrack and a list of suggested movies to accompany this book.